Christ, Christianity, & The Catholic Religion

My Personal Experience With Jehovah

By Joseph C. Whyte

ISBN: 0-615-14596-5
ISBN-13: 978-0-6151-4596-9
Libraty Of Congress Control Numbet: 2007903498

Printed in the United States of America

To order additional copies, please contact us.
BookSurge, LLC
www.booksurge.com
1-866-308-6235

All Scripture quotations are taken from the following
versions of the Holy Bible and are indicated
throughout this book by the abbreviations listed:

KJV - King James Version
BBE - Bible in Basic English
CEV - Contemporary English Version
ASV - American Standard Version

To Pauline Whyte,
My beloved wife, friend,
and confidant of 18 years.
You are my gift from God and
I'm blessed to have you as
my life companion.

Table of Contents

Table of Contents - continued

I

The Dreams

Iwas a teenager approaching my seventeenth birthday when I had the first dream. It was the weekend and I had been out with my friends until the early morning hours. I had gotten into bed a little after 2:00 a.m. and had fallen asleep when in my dream I found myself back in high school. School was out and I was enjoying my summer vacation but in my dream I was at school on the football field, all alone and there was no one else there. I looked around as I stood there, not daring to move, and wondered aloud, "Why am I here? There is no school so why am I here?" As I said this out loud I noticed movement from behind the cafeteria building to my left and suddenly the silhouette of a man began moving towards me. I was not afraid and as the figure moved closer I began to recognize who it was.

"Robert Grant?" I asked more to myself than to him. I was surprised and a little shocked. You see, Robert Grant had been dead for several years. He was a school mate of mine who had died several years earlier. We were both in the ninth grade when it happened. He was just fifteen years old and I was fourteen at the time. We used to walk from school together each afternoon to the bus terminal located downtown Kingston, Jamaica. We would discuss all kinds of things as we walked; our topics ranged from girlfriends to what we would be when we grew up.

I remember our last walk and our last conversation as if it were yesterday. We were going home that afternoon and the conversation was about girls. We were teenage boys and our fascination with members of the opposite sex was quite normal. We spoke quite a lot about girls and women. As we walked along we passed a group of people preaching and singing in the St. William Grant Park, the largest park downtown. They were clapping their hands, singing, and beating tambourines. There would be intermittent pauses in their singing during which time they would preach about Jesus, salvation, and the last judgment of God.

In Jamaica, this is not unusual; in fact it is quite common. Because it is so common, we never really stop to listen. For some odd reason, today was different. Robert grabbed me by the hand as we were about to walk by and said, "Let's listen for a while." We stopped just before the group of preachers and singers, and along with a few other people who had done the same, listened for awhile. Robert listened intently, showing a great amount of interest in what was being said. I, on the other hand, just wanted to leave. I was never comfortable with hearing about Jesus and hell. It was troublesome to me and I just wanted not to think about such things. After being satisfied, he started walking away and I walked along with him. It was then that he said the words that I will never forget for the rest of my life. He said, "Before I die I must be a Christian." He said it more to himself than to me. As if unaware of what he had just said, he suddenly changed the subject of the conversation and we started a lively discussion about our favorite topic, women.

We parted company on this the last day of school; the summer holiday break had begun. I fully expected to see him in September, the beginning of the new school year. This was, however, the last time I would see Robert Grant. He died of a gunshot wound that summer. He was not a Christian.

Why was Robert Grant in my dream? Why were we here together alone in school with no one else? As he got closer to me I asked him, "What are you doing here? You are dead!" He looked at me with an expressionless face and simply replied, "They sent me back to warn you."

"Warn me about what?" I asked.

"They sent me to warn you so that you'll not end up where I am because it is not lovely," he responded.

I was frightened and struggled to wake out of my dream. I woke up in a sweat and I was scared. The following morning I met my friends and told them about the dream. My friends would come to my house each morning and we would plan our nocturnal outing for the coming night. After hearing the dream they all laughed and suggested that I may have had just one too many beers. I had just started drinking and alcohol was new to me. In a strange way I was comforted by their laughs and soon dismissed the entire thing from my thoughts. Yes, I said to myself, it had to be the beers.

I went out that night and had a great time. I went to bed approximately the same time as the night before and fell asleep shortly after. I had another dream. This time I was at school but on the senior campus. My high school is divided into two campuses, a junior campus that goes up to the ninth grade and a senior campus that goes up to grade thirteen. In the first dream I was on the junior campus. Except for the difference in the campus, the second dream was almost exactly as the first dream.

I was again standing in the middle of the football field and school was not in session so I was all alone. I asked myself the same questions, "Why am I here? There is no school so why am I here?" As I stood there bewildered, I looked over towards the basketball court and saw movement. Someone was coming towards me. Again it was Robert Grant.

I asked the same question I had asked in the previous dream. "What are you doing here? You are dead!" He responded the same as before, "They sent me back to warn you." This time I became bold in the dream and said to him, "This is not real because you are dead!" He then slowly turned around until his back was facing me and then asked, "What do you see on my back?" I looked carefully at his back. He was covered from his waist down but his upper body was naked. I saw cracks in his back like fissures that I could not explain. I said "There are cracks in your back!" He then turned around suddenly, and with a frightful stare shouted, "They put me back together so I could warn you, so you'll not end up where I am because it is not lovely here!"

With that, I woke up again in a sweat, and was quite shaken. I again informed my friends of the dream, expecting them to brush it off, but this time no one laughed. There was just silence, a fearful silence that was a bit eerie. "You are being warned," Paul said, "You should take it seriously." Paul was the oldest of the group and I was not particularly fond of him. I tried to dismiss his comment and he got upset. He said that if I refused to heed the warning then he would heed the warning in my place. That evening as we got ready to go out, Paul appeared dressed in a suit and tie with a Bible in hand. He informed us that he would no longer be going out with us as he was going to church. He wanted all of us to heed the warning of the dreams and go to church with him. We did not. Paul later became a born-again Christian and I heard that he died a few years later while on a church trip.

A few months had gone by since my last dream and I had not had another dream like those two since. My life had gone on and many positive things had occurred. I was back in school and had been elected editor of my school's yearbook. I was made captain of the school's debating team and represented the school in debates sponsored by UNESCO (United Nations Education, Scientific, and Cultural Organization). I was invited by the local TV station to debate students from other schools on a new national television program that had just been launched. Things were going well for me and I never gave the dreams a second thought, that is, until one fateful afternoon that changed my life.

As I did with Robert Grant a few years before, a group of friends and I would walk from school to the main bus terminal downtown. We would walk the streets that were free of traffic and would debate, sometimes boisterously, as we tackled issues from politics, to religion, to philosophy. This afternoon we were debating the differences between fate and faith. We had started the discussion in the school library and had continued it as we made our way downtown to the bus terminal. We were walking in the center of the street and there was no one around but us, a group of about five high school students wearing white shirts and khaki pants.

I remember very clearly being in the front of the group when suddenly a man appeared in the middle of the street with his back turned toward us. He was not there just a minute before. Where did he come from and why was he standing in the middle of the street with his back towards us? Did he not see us coming? Could he not hear us? These questions raced through my mind. As we approached him, he suddenly spun around, pointed at me and said, "I've been sent to warn you of the iron and clay!"

I thought this man was out of his mind. I immediately looked him over very quickly. His clothes were clean. His hair was not well groomed; he wore it high like an afro and though his clothes were clean they were not neatly pressed.

I thought it safe to engage him in debate as clearly he was not insane. I spun around to my colleagues and indicated that we take him on about this warning. Maybe we could humiliate him in debate. At least that was my plan. As I turned again to face him, I received the shock of my life as there was no one standing before me. He had literally disappeared before a group of five students.

I turned to the group and they were all frozen in their tracks; had we just seen what we had seen? How could a man be there one minute and not there the next? We were stunned into silence and there was an air of unease. We stood our ground for a moment, silent, not knowing what to make of what just happened. Someone said, "Maybe he ran down to the intersection." This was not possible; the intersection was about a quarter mile from where we stood. One of us ran down to the intersection but there was no one there. We were still the only occupants of the street. We were all visibly shaken. What was this warning and what did iron and clay mean? We were afraid and speechless.

The following day at school we all came together to discuss the strange and frightening occurrence. We desperately wanted to know what was meant by "iron and clay" and this preoccupied our thoughts and discussions for the better part of the day. One student eventually found the key to the mystery in the Bible. We were not religious by any measure. I was not raised in a church and could not recall having even visited a church in many, many years. The truth was that churches made me uncomfortable. There was so much emphasis on being saved and giving your life to Jesus that I had no interest in church. All I wanted was to enjoy the world and to taste of all its offerings. Church and Jesus were not factored into my future plans. The Bible did not hold my interest and I remember jokingly dismissing a fellow student who tried speaking to me about God with the question, "All my friends will be in hell, so why would I want to go to heaven?"

The discovery of this mystery phrase in the Bible suddenly changed all that. The dreams I had about Robert Grant came rushing back and I desperately wanted to know what this phrase meant. What does the "iron and clay" mean and why was this person or being sent to warn us about it? The phrase was found in a verse in the Old Testament book of Daniel, *"Thou sawest till that a stone was cut out without hands, which smote the image upon his feet that were of iron and clay, and brake them to pieces."(KJV, Daniel 2:34)*, and speaks about Nebuchadnezzar's dream. Nebuchadnezzar was the then king of a city named Babylon and Jehovah had given him a dream. No one could interpret the dream but the prophet Daniel. In his dream, Nebuchadnezzar saw a great image whose feet were of iron and clay. Daniel explained that the feet being of part iron and part clay represented the world at its end. Iron does not stick to clay and so the world will be fragmented and divided at the time of the end.

It was all too much for me and I began fearing for my very life. This was my third warning. Two warnings in my dreams and now this warning from an event I could not rationally explain. I started questioning myself. What if Robert were truly in hell and was truly sent back to warn me? What was the purpose of this life? Why was I here and why was I even born? I needed answers and I needed them fast. I recounted the things of the world that I had experimented with. I had started going out to clubs, I had started drinking, I tried smoking, and I now had a serious girlfriend.

As I recounted these activities, I concluded that life had to hold more than just drinking, going out and having fun, and engaging oneself in relationships. If this was all there was, life was pointless, I concluded.

My search for truth, for meaning to life and for God had started. It was during this search that I came across a nugget of truth that gave me direction. I found it in the Encyclopedia Britannica and it was the story of Emperor Constantine of Rome, the Christian religion, and the Sabbath day. I immediately started asking if there were churches that held services on Saturdays instead of Sundays. It was then that I was introduced to a schoolmate named John Birch who informed me that he attended a church that met on Saturdays.

I became a born-again Christian approximately six months later and finally started finding the answers I was looking for. I also found many things I had not set out to look for. I found that not all religious people were interested in truth and many are not in search of answers. This book identifies many of the truths I have found and also many falsehoods I discovered along the way.

It outlines my personal walk with Jehovah, my spiritual development, and my need to communicate the warnings I received to anyone who reads this book. In this book I present the truth of Christianity as I've found it through twenty four years of relationship with Jesus and through twenty four years of studying the Holy Scriptures.

2

The Christian Religion

The Christian religion is based on the teachings of Jesus the Christ, the son of the living God, Jehovah, as outlined in the Holy Bible. The Holy Bible includes both the Old and New Testaments. The teachings of the Holy Bible, the doctrines as outlined from the book of Genesis to the book of Revelation and no other book, are the foundation of the Christian religion. This is the fundamental truth that distinguishes Christianity from all other religions. All other doctrines and religious rituals that are outside of the context of the Holy Scriptures, even if incorporated into the mainstream Christian churches, are essentially non-Christian.

This is the reason why celebrations and festivals such as Christmas and Easter are non-Christian festivals. We will see more examples of non-Christian festivals and celebrations that are practiced in today's mainstream Christian churches as we further examine the Christian religion. As we explore what Christianity is within the confines of the definition provided us by Jehovah, Jesus, the Apostles, and the prophets of Jehovah, we will discover that many current practices that are labeled as Christian are in fact not.

Christianity can be summed up very simply as the religion of Jehovah and Jesus His only begotten son. It is a religion of one God, Jehovah, who manifested himself in human flesh so that He could be nailed to a cross and die. His death, burial, and resurrection from the dead provide the source of hope for all humanity as it represents a victory over death and over sin. Thus, the Christian lives with the eternal knowledge that physical death is not the final judgment on mankind but that death has been defeated and the door to salvation and eternal life has been opened unto us.

Christianity only exists because of the existence of sin. Without sin there would be no need for a savior and salvation would be wholly unnecessary. Sin, though not a popular subject among many religious groups, is the only reason for salvation. Human beings are sinful and are guilty of sin from the time of birth. This is stated clearly in the Holy Scriptures and we will examine these scriptures as we further dicuss the Christian religion.

Sin, as defined in the Holy Scriptures, is a violation of the Laws Jehovah has outlined for believers to follow in order to access the salvation that has been presented to us through the death and resurrection of His Son Jesus the Christ. Yes, Laws. The very mention of laws is oftentimes greeted with hostility in today's religious communities; however, there would be no Christianity without laws, laws created not by humans but laws that are written and instituted by Jehovah himself.

The New Testament book of I Timothy 1:9-11 outlines why laws are necessary, *"We also understand that it [the law] wasn't given to control people who please God, but to control lawbreakers, criminals, godless people, and sinners. It is for wicked and evil people, and for murderers, who would even kill their own parents. The Law was written for people who are sexual perverts or who live as homosexuals or are kidnappers or liars or won't tell the truth in court. It is for anything else that opposes the correct teaching of the good news that the glorious and wonderful God has given..." (CEV)*

Because we are all guilty of being sinners, laws are an absolute necessity in our lives and our relationship with Jehovah; it cannot be otherwise. Our look at the Christian religion will cover the following pertinent topics:

- Who is Jesus?

- The Apostles of Jesus

- The Christian Doctrine - Grace, Works, and Laws

- The Personal Relationship with Jesus

- Death, Burial, Resurrection & The Coming Judgment

- The Catholic Religion

This comprehensive look at the Christian religion will be based only on what the Holy Scriptures state and not on the works, opinions, or commentaries of any individual.

3

Who Is Jesus?

T o understand who Jesus is, it is necessary to examine what Jesus had to say about himself. In the book of John 8:58, Jesus says of himself, *"I tell you for certain that even before Abraham was, I was, and I am." (CEV)* Abraham is the father of the people of Israel, commonly referred to today as Jews. To understand who Jesus is, it is necessary to go back to Abraham and beyond. Though Jesus is referred to in the Holy Scriptures as the *"Seed of Abraham"* and as the *"Son of David"* (Matthew 1:1 & Hebrews 2:16), He is truly only the Son of God and also God manifested in the flesh. We will see later on why He is called these additional names. Jesus is Jehovah. He is not another God that works along with Jehovah or agrees in principle with Jehovah. He does not sit on a board of directors with Jehovah and discuss matters with Jehovah. He *is* Jehovah. This may seem a little confusing to the average person; however, it will be made clear as we look into the deity of Jesus.

To understand who Jesus is, we must begin at the creation, before life existed on this earth. The book of Genesis records how Jehovah created all things in six literal days and rested on the seventh day. He blessed the seventh day, made it holy, and called it the Sabbath day. This fact will become very important to us later on. Genesis 1:1-2 records the creation event, *"In the beginning God created the heavens and the earth. The earth was barren, with no form of life; it was under a roaring ocean covered with darkness. But the Spirit of God was moving over the water." (CEV)* The same event, the creation of the earth, is also recorded in the New Testament Gospel of John 1:1-4, *"In the beginning was the one who is called the Word. The Word was with God and was truly God. From the very beginning the Word was with God. And with this Word, God created all things. Nothing was made without the Word. Everything that was created received its life from him, and his life gave light to everyone."(CEV)*

Comparing these two recorded versions of the creation of the Earth, we see that God (Jehovah) created the heavens and the earth in the book of Genesis. We also see from the book of John that all things were created by the *"Word,"* which is a reference to Jesus, the Son of God. This tells us that Jesus existed from the beginning before there existed life and that all life that now exists, exist because He created it. Jesus in essence is the Creator. This agrees with Jesus' earlier statement that *"before Abraham was, I was."*

It is important to pay keen attention to the fact that the Apostle John not only describes Jesus as being with God but also as being God: *"The Word was with God and was truly God."* Jesus is truly Jehovah manifested as a human being so He could die on a cross and give salvation to humanity. Further in the book of John, chapter 1:14 it states: *"The Word became a human being and lived here with us."* From these scriptures we can arrive at several important conclusions:

1. God (Jehovah) created the heavens and the earth as stated in the book of Genesis. All things that exist were created by Him in six days and He rested on the seventh day.

2. From the book of John we see that Jesus (the Word) created all things in the beginning. There is nothing that exists that was not created by Him.

3. Since Jehovah created all things and all things are also created by Jesus, then it is inevitable that we conclude that Jesus and Jehovah are one and the same.

4. Jesus (the Word) became a human being and lived here on the earth.

5. Since Jesus (the Word) created all things and also became a human being and lived on earth, the inevitable conclusion is that Jehovah (God, creator of all things), lived here on the earth as a human being. This again leads to the conclusion that Jesus and Jehovah are one and the same.

There is further compelling evidence throughout the Holy Scriptures to support the fact that Jehovah (Yahweh, the God of Israel), is also Jesus the Son of God. The Gospel of Matthew records the event that announced the coming birth of Jesus to a young virgin named Mary. She was engaged to be married to a man named Joseph. Joseph discovered that Mary was pregnant, and knowing that he was not the father of the child, he contemplated cancelling the engagement privately so that he might not cause her any embarrassment.

While he thought about doing this, an angel of Jehovah appeared unto him and spoke the following words, '*"Joseph, the baby that Mary will have is from the Holy Spirit. Go ahead and marry her. Then after her baby is born, name him Jesus, because he will save his people from their sins." So the Lord's promise came true, just as the prophet had said, "A virgin will have a baby boy, and he will be called Immanuel," which means "God is with us."' (CEV, Matthew 1:20-23)*

Note that Jesus is described by the angel as *"God is with us."* Jesus was truly Jehovah in flesh. Further evidence is found in the book of the prophet Isaiah who prophesied about the coming of the Messiah, Jesus. In Isaiah chapter 9:6 he prophesies, *"A child has been born for us. We have been given a son who will be our ruler. His names will be Wonderful Advisor and Mighty God, Eternal Father and Prince of Peace."(CEV)* Echad

Here the prophet Isaiah refers to Jesus as *"Mighty God"* and *"Eternal Father"* in saying that a child shall be born to the nation of Israel. Jesus is the Eternal Father and the Mighty God. Surely there is no doubt that Jehovah is Jesus manifested in the flesh; however, conclusive evidence of Jesus being Jehovah comes from the lips of Jesus himself. In the New Testament book of John chapter 14:8, the Apostle Philip said to Jesus, *"Lord, show us the Father. That is all we need."(CEV)* Verse 9 of the same chapter records Jesus' response: *"Philip, I have been with you for a long time. Don't you know who I am? If you have seen me, you have seen the Father. How can you ask me to show you the Father?"(CEV)* are Echad

Jesus states clearly that He is indeed the Father, Jehovah, creator of all living things and creator of the world.

Since Jesus is then Jehovah, the God of Israel, why then is He called the Son of David and the seed of Abraham? The answer to this question is fairly simple. The scriptures describe Jehovah as being a spirit, *"God is Spirit. . ."* (John 4:24), and also makes clear that a spirit is not composed of flesh and bone as humans are. This is stated in the book of Luke 24:39: *". . .a spirit has not flesh and bones. . ."* Since a spirit cannot be crucified on a cross and blood is required to be shed for sin to be forgiven, God needed to come to the earth as a human sacrifice so that His blood could be shed for the remission or forgiveness of the sins of humans.

There are many today who find the thought of shedding blood to accomplish the forgiveness of sin to be repulsive indeed. Not only do they find it repulsive, they also believe it to be backward and barbaric. From the natural perspective, the carnal viewpoint of humanity, it does seem repulsive; however, from the spiritual perspective of God, it is not.

The New Testament book of Hebrews 9:22 clearly states that *". . .no sins can be forgiven unless blood is offered."(CEV)* It is precisely because blood is needed before sin can be forgiven that Jehovah had to be born as a human. In His state as a spirit, He does not have blood. Though blood has to be offered for the forgiveness of sin, not just any blood will do. The blood to be offered has to be from a sinless human being. This disqualifies all of humanity from being suitable as a sacrifice for sin.

The Holy Scriptures states that we are all born in sin. In other words, sin is programmed into our DNA before we are even born. This occurs through what I like to describe as spiritual inheritance. In the same way we inherit natural biological traits from our parents such as eye color, hair color, and natural abilities, we also inherit the spiritual condition called sin. Sin is our inherent tendency to violate the laws of God. We are programmed through this inheritance to do evil and not good. Good is not natural to humanity but evil certainly is. This is not difficult to understand; we just need to turn the television on and watch the evening news to see how evil the world is. Death, destruction, brutality, and savagery are all around us.

The Holy Scriptures explain in the New Testament book of Romans 5:12 how we all became sinners, *"Adam sinned, and that sin brought death into the world. Now everyone has sinned, and so everyone must die."(CEV)* Adam was the first human being Jehovah created and he is the father of all living human beings. He sinned against Jehovah and the resulting consequence of his sinful actions is that all his descendants, all peoples on the earth, are born in a state of sinfulness. To remedy this perpetual state of sin that humanity lived in, Jehovah had to sacrifice a sinless human. Sin came by the actions of man and therefore the solution to sin, a sinless sacrifice, had to come through the lineage of man.

This is the reason Jesus had to be born through the lineage of mankind. Jehovah could not just appear as a sinless man to be crucified. This would disqualify His sacrifice. Instead he had to be born into the human race as a man with a proven lineage. The only difference would be that the sperm of a sinful man would not be involved in His conception into the womb of a woman.

Jehovah chose the lineage of a man called Abraham (the father of the Jews), who obeyed Him and followed His instructions. He then established through Abraham's lineage a nation called Israel, which became known as the people of God. For this reason Jesus is often called the *"Seed of Abraham."* Israel had a great king, a king called David. King David became one of the greatest kings of the nation of Israel. Joseph, the husband of the virgin called Mary, was a descendant of King David of Israel and though he was not the biological father of Jesus, he was his father from the natural earthly perspective. This lineage makes Jesus a descendant of King David. This is the reason Jesus is often referred to as *"the Son of David."*

Jesus is, however, before his father Joseph, before King David, before Abraham, and before Adam. Jesus is Jehovah, the Eternal Father, The Mighty God, The Creator of all things, and because He was born for the purpose of dying as a sacrifice so that His sinless blood could be shed, He became known as the *"Lamb of God."* The New Testament book of John 1:29 describes Him as *"...the Lamb of God who takes away the sin of the world!"*

The inevitable challenge to the fact that Jesus is Jehovah comes in the form of the question, "If Jesus and Jehovah are one and the same, how do we explain Jesus praying to Jehovah while He was here on earth or how do we explain Jehovah declaring from heaven that Jesus is His beloved Son?"

There are many instances in the four New Testament Gospels where it is recorded that Jesus sought after Jehovah through prayer. One notable instance was just before Jesus' arrest while He prayed in the garden of Gethsemane. Here is the recorded text as presented by the Apostle Matthew in the book of Matthew 26:39, *"Jesus walked on a little way. Then he knelt with his face to the ground and prayed, "My Father, if it is possible, don't make me suffer by having me drink from this cup. But do what you want, and not what I want.""(CEV)*

Here we see Jesus praying to His father Jehovah and requesting reprieve from the coming crucifixion (*this cup*). Another notable instance is recorded in the book of John 17:1-3, *"After Jesus had finished speaking to his disciples, he looked up toward heaven and prayed: Father, the time has come for you to bring glory to your Son, in order that he may bring glory to you. And you gave him power over all people, so that he would give eternal life to everyone you give him. Eternal life is to know you, the only true God, and to know Jesus Christ, the one you sent."(CEV)*

In both instances we see Jesus, the Son of Jehovah, praying to Jehovah. How can they then be one? The answer is not simple and requires being capable of thinking spiritually and not naturally. In our natural world, no one can be in more than one place at any given time; we do not have a ubiquitous presence. With Jehovah, however, things are a lot different; He does have a ubiquitous presence. He is in all places at all times. This is recorded in the Old Testament book of Proverbs 15:3 *"The LORD sees everything, whether good or bad."(CEV)*

Jehovah can only see everything if He is everywhere at the same time. Jehovah is not limited as humans are. Here is what the book of I Timothy 3:16 says about Jesus being God, *"And without controversy great is the mystery of godliness: God was manifest in the flesh, justified in the Spirit, seen of angels, preached unto the Gentiles, believed on in the world, received up into glory."(KJV)*

The book of Timothy describes it as a mystery, that is, a truth that cannot be known except by revelation and cannot be fully understood. The mystery as stated here is that God (Jehovah) manifested Himself as a human being in the flesh (*God was manifest in the flesh*), pleased Himself by His actions here on earth as Jesus (*justified in the Spirit*), and was again received up into heaven after His resurrection from the dead (*received up into glory*).

From a natural human perspective, this will not make any sense at all. That is the reason why this mystery of Jehovah can only be understood spiritually. Thought of spiritually, however, it can be said that Jehovah sent a part of Himself down to earth as a sinless human to die for the sins of man while He maintained watch over Himself (Jesus) from heaven. He was also on every continent, in every country, in every home, seeing everyone's thoughts, and hearing every word spoken by every human being at the same time.

Clearly this makes no sense to the natural mind but to the spiritual mind it is not only true, it is expected. That is the reason we call Him God. Jesus then is the manifestation of Jehovah and Jehovah is Jesus manifested.

4

The Apostles Of Jesus

Jesus began his ministry on earth by being baptized by John the Baptist. He was then led by the Holy Spirit into the desert to be tested by the Devil, known throughout the Holy Scriptures as the Serpent, the Evil One, and also as Satan. To prepare for the Devil's tests or temptations, Jesus went without food and water for forty days and forty nights. This is also known as a fast. This was spiritual preparation so that He could encounter and successfully prevail against the most evil of spiritual forces known to the Earth.

After successfully resisting all the temptations of the Devil, Jesus began recruiting men whom He called Apostles. The book of Matthew 4:17–20, records the recruiting of the first Apostles: *"Then Jesus started preaching, "Turn back to God! The kingdom of heaven will soon be here." While Jesus was walking along the shore of Lake Galilee, he saw two brothers. One was Simon, also known as Peter, and the other was Andrew. They were fishermen, and they were casting their net into the lake. Jesus said to them, "Come with me! I will teach you how to bring in people instead of fish." Right then, the two brothers dropped their nets and went with him. Jesus walked on until he saw James and John, the sons of Zebedee. They were in a boat with their father, mending their nets. Jesus asked them to come with him too. Right away they left the boat and their father and went with Jesus."(CEV)*

Jesus went on to recruit twelve Apostles. The names of the twelve Apostles are listed below:

1. Simon Peter

2. Andrew - Simon Peter's brother

3. James - the son of Zebedee

4. John - the son of Zebedee

5. Philip

6. Thomas

7. Bartholomew

8. Matthew (the Tax Collector)

9. James of Alphaeus

10. Simon Zelotes

11. Judas (also known as Jude and Lebbaeus Thaddaeus)

12. Judas Iscariot (The one who betrayed Christ)

The twelve Apostles are extremely important to the Christian religion as they are the ones who received first-hand training from Jesus. They were prepared by Jesus for approximately three and a half years for the proclaiming of the Christian Gospel to the world. For three and a half years Jesus taught them about the coming kingdom of God, revealed to them that He would be crucified for the sins of humanity, and also that He would be resurrected from the dead. He further revealed to them significant future events that would occur in the nation of Israel and the world. Jesus also spoke about signs to look for that will indicate the approaching end of the world as it currently is, about persecutions to come, about forgiving their fellow men, and about loving each other.

Indeed, without the twelve Apostles, there would not be a New Testament Bible as the New Testament Bible is a collection of the writings and letters of the Apostles. There are two additional Apostles that are not listed in the original list of Apostles. The first is Matthias, who was selected by the remaining eleven Apostles after Judas, who betrayed Jesus, had committed suicide, and the second is the Apostle Paul, formerly known as Saul, who was selected by Jesus Himself, after the resurrection and ascension into heaven.

The selection of the Apostle Paul deserves attention before we move on to the further importance of the Apostles in the Christian religion. The Apostle Paul was at first an enemy of the infant church. He was a persecutor of the believers in Christ and approved of their murder and imprisonment. He was a leading figure in the attempted destruction of the spreading of the new Gospel. The book of Acts 9:1-6 records the unusual call of Paul (formerly Saul) to be an Apostle of Jesus Christ, *"Saul kept on threatening to kill the Lord's followers. He even went to the high priest and asked for letters to the Jewish leaders in Damascus. He did this because he wanted to arrest and take to Jerusalem any man or woman who had accepted the Lord's Way. When Saul had almost reached Damascus, a bright light from heaven suddenly flashed around him. He fell to the ground and heard a voice that said, "Saul! Saul! Why are you so cruel to me?" "Who are you?" Saul asked. "I am Jesus," the Lord answered. "I am the one you are so cruel to. Now get up and go into the city, where you will be told what to do."(CEV)*

This dramatic incident outlines the call of Saul to be an Apostle of Jesus. He was later to be known as the Apostle Paul instead of Saul. Saul's conversion to the Christian religion had far-reaching effects upon the spreading of the Christian Gospel throughout the world. Later we will see the impact that his ministry had on the spreading of Christianity in a largely pagan society.

The Resurrection & the Commission

After Jesus' crucifixion, just as He had prophesied to the Apostles, He was resurrected after three days and three nights. The resurrection of Jesus from the dead is an area that needs our attention for just a few moments. It is important that we recognize that Jesus was dead, not in a coma, for three complete days and three complete nights. We will look at the prophecies outlined in the Holy Scriptures regarding this time period to determine when Jesus was crucified, how long He remained dead and buried, and when He was resurrected.

This is important because there are many conflicting, confusing, and erroneous teachings regarding this that are not supported by the Holy Scriptures. As stated before, the sole source of truth that is being relied on for this book is the Holy Scriptures. It is the only authority that we have on the Christian religion. Let us therefore examine the Biblical facts about Jesus' death.

In the New Testament book of John 2:19-22, Jesus in foretelling of His death and resurrection from the dead said, *"Destroy this temple... and in three days I will build it again!" The leaders replied, "It took forty-six years to build this temple. What makes you think you can rebuild it in three days?" But Jesus was talking about his body as a temple. And when he was raised from death, his disciples remembered what he had told them. Then they believed the Scriptures and the words of Jesus."(CEV)*

Here we see Jesus informing His Apostles that He would be dead for three complete twenty-four hour days, not partial days, but whole days. In the New Testament book of Matthew, Jesus also makes clear the time period for which He would be dead. The Jewish leaders were not accepting of the fact that He was the Son of Jehovah and asked Him for a sign to prove that He was. Jesus responded in Matthew 12:39-40, *"You want a sign because you are evil and won't believe! But the only sign you will get is the sign of the prophet Jonah. He was in the stomach of a big fish for three days and nights, just as the Son of Man will be deep in the earth for three days and nights."* Here again we see Jesus confirming that He would be dead for a complete seventy two hour period before His resurrection.

Christian tradition celebrates what is called Easter, which truly is a non-Christian festival. During this festival there is what is known as *"Good Friday"* or the day of Jesus' crucifixion. There is also what is known as *"Resurrection Sunday,"* the day this festival claims Jesus was resurrected from the dead. There is just one problem with these festival days and it is that the time period between them does not total to three days and three nights as stated in the Holy Scriptures.

It is truly mind-boggling that otherwise very intelligent people will accept the falsehood that Jesus died on a Friday and was resurrected on the following Sunday and accomplished three days and three nights in the grave. They offer explanations such as partial days being counted as whole days and that Jesus did not truly mean a seventy two hour time period.

It only requires the ability to do simple calculations to determine that the period between Friday afternoon and Sunday morning could not be three days and three nights. Let us outline the calculations in the following points:

1. If Jesus died on a Friday afternoon and was buried before the sunset of the same day, then Friday night would be His first night in the grave. This gives us 1 night.

2. Saturday would then be His first day in the grave. This gives us 1 day. Thus far we are up to 1 night and 1 day.

3. Saturday night would be His second night in the grave. This gives us 2 nights. Thus far we are up to 2 nights and 1 day.

4. A Sunday morning resurrection gives us a grand total of 2 nights and 1 day in the grave. This is a far cry from the 3 days and the 3 nights that Jesus prophesied.

Since we know that Jesus is Jehovah and that He cannot lie (this is stated in the Old Testament book of Numbers 23:19, *"God is no mere human! He doesn't tell lies or change his mind. God always keeps his promises* , then we should search for the truth in the Holy Scriptures.

Since Jehovah cannot lie, then the error is on the part of the creators of the festival. How then could they have made such an error in calculating three days and three nights? The error begins with confusion about the day Christ was crucified. Jesus was not crucified on a Friday as is so commonly believed but on a Wednesday or, as the Holy Scriptures point out, the middle of the week. Surprised? Do not be. The Holy Scriptures are clear.

Another mistake that is made in the calculation is the erroneous belief that Jesus was resurrected from the dead on Sunday morning. He was not. Instead Jesus was resurrected from the dead at the end of the Sabbath. This would be sunset on Saturday. Let us redo the calculations from the Wednesday to sunset on Saturday to see if we arrive at the three days and three nights that Jesus stated.

I. Jesus was crucified on Wednesday during the day and was buried Wednesday evening before the sunset. Wednesday night would be his first night in the grave. Thus we have 1 night in the grave.

2. Thursday would be His first day in the grave. Thus we have 1 night and 1 day in the grave.

3. Thursday night would be His second night in the grave. Thus we have 2 nights and 1 day in the grave.

4. Friday would be His second day in the grave. This gives us 2 nights and 2 days in the grave.

5. Friday night would be his third night in the grave. This gives us <u>3</u> nights and <u>2</u> days in the grave.

6. Saturday would be His third day in the grave. This gives us <u>3</u> nights and <u>3</u> days in the grave.

7. Jesus was resurrected at the end of the Sabbath day, which is sunset on Saturday. He therefore spent a complete seventy two hour period in the grave and fulfilled His own prophecy.

Now that we have outlined the simple mathematics of His death and resurrection, let us turn to the Holy Scriptures for the necessary evidence. We know the truth must be contained in the Scriptures as it is our only source of truth. We did not simply count backwards to arrive at a Wednesday crucifixion. The information is actually found in the Holy Scriptures. Since the Holy Scriptures also state in Romans 3:4 that, "...*God tells the truth, even if everyone else is a liar,*" we must first accept that it is an impossibility that Jesus was crucified on a Friday and resurrected on a Sunday morning.

This is the first step in looking for truth. The lie must be recognized and rejected as a falsehood. We will now begin our search for the truth by looking at a few important points that have been overlooked. We begin in the Old Testament with the Jewish feast called the Passover and also at the many Jewish Sabbaths.

The Passover & the Sabbaths

Our search for the truth does not begin in the New Testament and the account of the crucifixion as many might expect, but in the Old Testament. We are interested particularly in the Hebrew festival called the Passover and also in the weekly Sabbath.

Let's begin with the Sabbath Day. In the book of Exodus 20: 8-11, Jehovah reminds the Israelites about the Sabbath day, *"Remember that the Sabbath Day belongs to me. You have six days when you can do your work, but the seventh day of each week belongs to me, your God. No one is to work on that day--not you, your children, your slaves, your animals, or the foreigners who live in your towns. In six days I made the sky, the earth, the oceans, and everything in them, but on the seventh day I rested. That's why I made the Sabbath a special day that belongs to me."(CEV)*

The Sabbath day is a Holy day for the people of Israel and for all Christians. During the time of the Sabbath, only worship and rest are permitted. The day belongs to Jehovah. This is the weekly Sabbath that was established by Jehovah and begins at sunset on a Friday and completes at sunset on Saturday evening. During this period the Christian believer is required to worship Jehovah and rest from all work. We will see the importance of this weekly Sabbath as it relates to the calculations previously outlined.

There is also the festival or celebration of the Passover that Jehovah commanded the Israelites to observe each year in celebration of their deliverance from slavery in Egypt. The Hebrews had been the slaves of the Egyptians for approximately 400 years before Jehovah delivered them from Egyptian bondage. This deliverance was preceded by a series of miracles, done through Moses, that are known as the *"Ten Plagues."* The final of these Ten Plagues was the killing of the firstborn, both human and animal, of the Egyptians. Jehovah commanded Moses to establish the feast of the Passover among the Israelites so that their firstborn would not be harmed during that period. This plague resulted in the death of Pharaoh's son, and in his heartbroken state, he commanded that the Israelites be free to leave Egypt.

The Passover was to be celebrated on the fourteenth day of the first month according to the Hebrew calendar and on the fifteenth day following the Passover, there would be no work done as this began the celebrating of another holy Hebrew feast, the Feast of Unleavened Bread. This is outlined in the following scripture Leviticus 23:5-7, *"In the first month, on the fourteenth day of the month at nightfall, is the Lord's Passover; And on the fifteenth day of the same month is the feast of unleavened bread; for seven days let your food be unleavened bread. On the first day you will have a holy meeting; you may do no sort of field-work."*

It is important to note that on the first day of the Feast of Unleavened Bread, which is the first day after the Passover, the Israelites are not permitted to work, similar to the ban on work previously outlined in the weekly Sabbath. This is of great importance as many Christians mistakenly believe that the only Sabbath that Jehovah commanded the Israelites to observe was the weekly Sabbath that commences at sunset on Friday and end at sunset on Saturday.

Whenever God required the Israelites to cease from work and to observe a feast in His honor or to offer special sacrifices for the sins of the people, Jehovah would make that particular day or days a Sabbath or Sabbaths. These Sabbaths are separate from the weekly Sabbath outlined in the Ten Commandments. It is very important that this be clearly understood. Here are several scriptures that demonstrate this:

Leviticus 23:23-25:

> "And the LORD spake unto Moses, saying, Speak unto the children of Israel, saying, In the seventh month, in the first day of the month, shall ye have a **Sabbath**, a memorial of blowing of trumpets, an holy convocation. Ye shall do no servile work therein: but ye shall offer an offering made by fire unto the LORD." (KJV)

Leviticus 23:39:

> "Also in the fifteenth day of the seventh month, when ye have gathered in the fruit of the land, ye shall keep a feast unto the LORD seven days: on the first day shall be a **Sabbath**, and on the eighth day shall be a **Sabbath**." (KJV)

Leviticus 16:29-31:

> "And this shall be a statute for ever unto you: that in the seventh month, on the tenth day of the month, ye shall afflict your souls, and do no work at all, whether it be one of your own country, or a stranger that sojourneth among you: For on that day shall the priest make an atonement for you, to cleanse you, that ye may be clean from all your sins before the LORD. It shall be a **Sabbath** of rest unto you, and ye shall afflict your souls, by a statute for ever." (KJV)

It becomes evident from these scriptures that the word *"Sabbath"* in the Holy Scriptures does not always make reference to the seventh-day weekly Sabbath found in the Ten Commandments. The word Sabbath also makes reference to any day or in some cases year, that Jehovah commands the Israelites to observe a festival, appear before Him for atonement, or for the land to rest. This is the case with the day after the festival of the Passover, known as the Feast of the Passover.

The Passover is observed on the fourteenth day of the first month of Nisan, according to the Hebrew calendar and the fifteenth day is *a Sabbath* to the Israelites. No work can be done on that day. The Old Testament book of Leviticus 23:5-7 makes this clear, *"In the fourteenth day of the first month at even is the LORD'S Passover. And on the fifteenth day of the same month is the feast of unleavened bread unto the LORD: seven days ye must eat unleavened bread. In the first day ye shall have an holy convocation:* **ye shall do no servile work therein."** *(KJV)*

Here are the same verses from the Contemporary English Version (CEV) Bible:

"Passover is another time when you must come together to worship me, and it must be celebrated on the evening of the fourteenth day of the first month of each year. The Festival of Thin Bread begins on the fifteenth day of that same month; it lasts seven days, and during this time you must honor me by eating bread made without yeast. On the first day of this festival you must **rest from your work** *and come together for worship."*

Now that we have seen from the Holy Scriptures that the day after the Passover, the fifteenth day was a Sabbath unto the Israelites, not the seventh day Sabbath that comes after Friday, we can understand why many mistakenly believe Jesus was crucified on a Friday. Jesus was crucified on the fourteenth day, the day of the Passover. The following day, which began at sunset on the fourteenth day, was the fifteenth day and the first day of the Feast of Unleavened Bread. This was a Sabbath to the Israelites, a day during which they could do no work.

To completely understand the significance and importance of this, we need to also look at the beginning and ending of a day according to the Hebrew calendar. The Scriptures tell us that the beginning of a day is at sunset. Our calendar, based on the Roman tradition, has the beginning of the day at midnight. While reading the Holy Scriptures, it is very important to keep in mind that discussion about the days of the Passover and other festivals are not according to the Roman tradition of when a day begins and ends but after the Hebrew tradition. For instance, Saturday, the weekly Sabbath, begins Friday night according to Hebrew calendar.

To simplify our understanding of this we need only remember that the night is actually the beginning of the next day. The following will help in understanding this:

1. Monday actually begins Sunday at sunset.

2. Tuesday actually begins Monday at sunset.

3. Wednesday actually begins Tuesday at sunset.

4. Thursday actually begins Wednesday at sunset.

5. Friday actually begins Thursday at sunset.

6. Saturday (the weekly Sabbath) actually begins Friday at sunset.

7. Sunday actually begins Saturday at sunset.

This fact, which relates an understanding of the beginning of a day and the end of a day is important to establish when the Passover was actually eaten by Jesus and the Apostles. Since we know Jesus was crucified on a Wednesday (we'll soon look at the actual prophecy that foretold this), and He was arrested on the night of the Passover (remember the Passover is only eaten at night), it follows that Jesus then ate the Passover with His Apostles on what we would today consider to be Tuesday night, which in fact would be Wednesday evening.

This may be just a little difficult to grasp at first and you may ask yourself, "Does the night come before the day?" If in fact you asked yourself that question, then the answer is in the affirmative. In other words, YES! The order of the day was established by Jehovah in the book of Genesis at the time of the creation. After creating something, Jehovah recorded the day. Here are the scriptures that demonstrate this:

Genesis 1:1-19

*"The earth was barren, with no form of life; it was under a roaring ocean covered with darkness. But the Spirit of God was moving over the water. God said, "I command light to shine!" And light started shining. God looked at the light and saw that it was good. He separated light from darkness and named the light "Day" and the darkness "Night." **Evening came and then morning--that was the first day."***

*God said, "I command a dome to separate the water above it from the water below it." And that's what happened. God made the dome and named it "Sky." **Evening came and then morning--that was the second day.***

*God said, "I command the water under the sky to come together in one place, so there will be dry ground." And that's what happened. God named the dry ground "Land," and he named the water "Ocean." God looked at what he had done and saw that it was good. God said, "I command the earth to produce all kinds of plants, including fruit trees and grain." And that's what happened. The earth produced all kinds of vegetation. God looked at what he had done, and it was good. **Evening came and then morning--that was the third day.***

*God said, "I command lights to appear in the sky and to separate day from night and to show the time for seasons, special days, and years. I command them to shine on the earth." And that's what happened. God made two powerful lights, the brighter one to rule the day and the other to rule the night. He also made the stars. Then God put these lights in the sky to shine on the earth, to rule day and night, and to separate light from darkness. God looked at what he had done, and it was good. **Evening came and then morning--that was the fourth day."(CEV)***

From these scriptures we see very clearly that the night of the day comes before the daylight portion of the day.

We have so far established the following:

1. The seventh day weekly Sabbath is just one of the many Sabbaths that are mentioned in the Holy Scriptures.

2. The concept of a day in the Holy Scriptures differs from the Roman concept of a day in that the evening or night of the day precedes the daylight portion of the day.

3. Jesus could not have been crucified on a Friday as it is mathematically impossible to obtain *3 days* and *3 nights* from Friday evening to Sunday morning.

4. The resurrection of Jesus was not on a Sunday morning.

Earlier, I mentioned that the Holy Scriptures prophesied the day of Jesus' crucifixion. This is our final piece of Biblical evidence to show without doubt that Jesus was crucified in the middle of the week or on a Wednesday.

Before we get to the actual scripture, however, let us refresh ourselves on the reason for Jesus coming to Earth to be crucified. Jesus is described as the Lamb of God and came so that He could be sacrificed and His blood shed for the forgiveness of the sins of humanity. We have seen earlier in the scriptures that there is no forgiveness of sin without the shedding of blood.

Prior to the coming of Jesus, Jehovah required that the Israelites offer sacrifices of bullocks, goats, and turtle doves as a way to atone for their sin. These sacrificial rituals were outlined in what became known as the Law of Moses. The Law of Moses is so called not because Moses invented the laws but because God instructed him to write the laws as He, Jehovah, dictated them to him.

This is the major difference between the Law of Moses and the Ten Commandments. Jehovah Himself wrote the Ten Commandments on two tables of stone with His own finger and gave them to Moses. The additional laws and rituals were afterward dictated to Moses and he had to write them down with His own hand.

Why is there significance to this? There is great significance to this because the Law of Moses was temporary while laws of the Ten Commandments are permanent. Jehovah, in His wisdom, knew that until Jesus was sacrificed for all sin, there would need to be an intermediary solution to the problem of sin. The Law of Moses served this intermediary purpose. The Israelites had to perform these sacrifices continually and had to appear before the priest who would then perform various rites contained in the Law of Moses for the sins of the people.

The Apostle Paul, in the New Testament book of Galatians chapter 3:24, in speaking about the Law of Moses, describes it as a servant that was necessary until we received Christ and learned to have faith through Jesus, *"So the law has been a servant to take us to Christ, so that we might have righteousness by faith. But now that faith is come, we are no longer under a servant. Because you are all sons of God through faith in Christ Jesus."(BBE)*

Here we see confirmation that the Law of Moses was temporary until the coming of Jesus and the sacrifice of Jesus. The Apostle Paul further expands his explanation on the purpose of the Law of Moses in the New Testament book of Hebrews 10:1-9, *"For the law, being only a poor copy of the future good things, and not the true image of those things, is never able to make the people who come to the altar every year with the same offerings completely clean. For if this had been possible, would there not have been an end of those offerings, because the worshippers would have been made completely clean and would have been no longer conscious of sins? But year by year there is a memory of sins in those offerings. Because it is not possible for the blood of oxen and goats to take away sins. So that when he comes into the world, he says, You had no desire for offerings, but you made a body ready for me; You had no joy in burned offerings or in offerings for sin. Then I said, See, I have come to do your pleasure, O God as it is said of me in the roll of the book. After saying, You had no desire for offerings, for burned offerings or offerings for sin which are made by the law and you had no pleasure in them, then he said, See, I have come to do your pleasure. **He took away the old order, so that he might put the new order in its place.**" (BBE)*

Here we see a more detailed description of the purpose of the Law of Moses and also how the sacrifice of Jesus as the Lamb of God, impacts these laws. The verse, *"He took away the old order, so that he might put the new order in its place,"* tells us clearly that Jesus' death would bring an end to the Law of Moses that required sacrifices and various offerings as atonement for sin.

Jesus would become the ultimate sacrifice and bring an end to all sacrifices for sin. Jehovah would no more accept any other offering for sin after the sacrifice of His Son Jesus. This fact is important to the establising of the day Jesus was crucified. The prophecy that states the day of His crucifixion makes mention of the ceasing of sacrifices that His death would bring about. The prophet Daniel prophesied about the death of Jesus. In the Old Testament book of Daniel 9:27, Daniel foretells the time of Jesus' death, *"...and in the midst of the week he shall cause the sacrifice and the oblation to cease..."*

As we have seen before, Jesus' death would result in an end to all Jewish sacrifices. The famous theologian Wesley makes this comment on the death of Jesus, *"By his death and blood shedding [He] shall cause the sacrifice to cease - All the Jewish rites, and Levitical worship. By his death he abrogated, and put an end to this laborious service, for ever."* The prophet Daniel makes mention of this end of religious sacrifices and also of the fact that it would occur in the middle of the week. The middle of the week is Wednesday and so we know that Jesus was crucified on a Wednesday.

Now that we have an understanding of this, let us recount the events leading up to the crucifixion of Jesus. Jesus sat with His Apostles and ate the Passover meal with them on the night of the Passover celebration. The Passover is eaten on the fourteenth day of the month of Nisan and is only eaten after sunset. This would then be what we today call Tuesday night, which in fact is the beginning of Wednesday. He was arrested after the Passover meal, tried on Wednesday, found guilty, and immediately crucified.

The coming sunset would mark the beginning of the Feast of unleavened bread. This would be *a Sabbath to the Jews* and they were forbidden to work on that day. It was not the weekly seventh-day

Sabbath, but one of the many Sabbaths that we've discussed before. This is clearly stated in the book of John 19:31, *"The Jews therefore, because it was the preparation, that the bodies should not remain upon the cross on the Sabbath day, (for that Sabbath day was an high day,) besought Pilate that their legs might be broken, and that they might be taken away."*

Note that the day of the crucifixion is called the "preparation." Because work cannot be done on the Sabbath, all preparation for the coming Sabbath had to be done the day prior to the Sabbath. For example, the Friday prior to the weekly seventh-day Sabbath (Saturday), is the day of preparation, when food has to be prepared and all work done before the Sabbath (sunset Friday) begins. The same preparation was occurring on the day of Jesus' crucifixion.

Jesus had to be taken down from the cross before sunset on Wednesday. He was placed in His tomb on Wednesday evening, just prior to sunset. He fulfilled the prophecy that He would be dead for three days and three nights, and was resurrected in the ending of the Sabbath. Thus, He was resurrected sunset on Saturday evening and not Sunday morning.

The Resurrection
& the Spiritual Body

The resurrection of Jesus is recorded in the four Gospels of the New Testament. It is the most important event to be recorded in the Bible as the resurrection of Jesus is what gives hope to the

Christian believer. If there were no resurrection then there would be no need for Christianity.

The resurrection of Jesus also distinguishes Christianity from all other world religions. Christ Jesus is the only human to have been resurrected from the dead and then to ascend into heaven. He was seen by many people, and as the Holy Scriptures state, by over five hundred at one time, many of whom were still alive at the writing of the New Testament book of I Corinthians.

We've already looked at when Jesus was resurrected and have determined that it was Saturday evening (the end of the Sabbath at sunset). We'll now look at the scriptures to support this fact and also at scriptures that demonstrate what happens to a resurrected body. Let us first begin by looking at what happened to Jesus' resurrected body. After His resurrection, Jesus was able to appear and disappear at will. He was able to enter closed buildings without going through a door and was also able to disguise His appearance from those close to Him. All this He did because He was resurrected with what the scriptures call a *"spiritual body."*

The book of I Corinthians 15:40-49 describes the fascinating transformation of the resurrected body, *"Everything in the heavens has a body, and so does everything on earth. But each one is very different from all the others. The sun isn't like the moon, the moon isn't like the stars, and each star is different. That's how it will be when our bodies are raised to life. These bodies will die, but the bodies that are raised will live forever. These ugly and weak bodies will become beautiful and strong. As surely as there are physical bodies, there are spiritual bodies. And our physical bodies will be changed into spiritual bodies. The first man was named Adam, and the Scriptures tell us that he was a living person. But Jesus, who may be called the last Adam, is a life-giving spirit. We see that the one with a spiritual body did not come first. He came after the one who had a physical body.*

The first man was made from the dust of the earth, but the second man came from heaven. Everyone on earth has a body like the body of the one who was made from the dust of the earth. And everyone in heaven has a body like the body of the one who came from heaven. Just as we are like the one who was made out of earth, we will be like the one who came from heaven."(CEV)

The point of this scripture is to demonstrate that a resurrected body is unlike the body that died. A resurrected body will be like the spiritual bodies in heaven. Jesus died with a natural body and was resurrected with a spiritual body.

As pointed out before, Jesus demonstrated what the resurrected body could do. The following scriptures taken from the book of John demonstrates His ability to enter a building without using a door or window. In both instances Jesus entered a building His Apostles were in by simply appearing in their midst:

"The disciples were afraid of the Jewish leaders, and on the evening of that same Sunday they locked themselves in a room. Suddenly, Jesus appeared in the middle of the group. He greeted them" (John 20:19, CEV)

"A week later the disciples were together again. This time, Thomas was with them. Jesus came in while the doors were still locked and stood in the middle of the group. He greeted his disciples" (John 20:26, CEV)

This demonstrated ability of the spiritual body to do things that cannot be done by the natural body is essential in explaining some controversial issues of the resurrection.

While it is already demonstrated that Jesus was not resurrected on a Sunday morning, there are many who point to the accounts of the resurrection in the four Gospels and dispute this fact. We will therefore present all four accounts of the resurrection of Jesus from the four Gospels for careful examination.

We begin in the book of Matthew. Here is Matthew's account of the resurrection of Jesus excerpted from Matthew 28:1-6:

"The Sabbath was over, and it was almost daybreak on Sunday when Mary Magdalene and the other Mary went to see the tomb. Suddenly a strong earthquake struck, and the Lord's angel came down from heaven. He rolled away the stone and sat on it. The angel looked as bright as lightning, and his clothes were white as snow. The guards shook from fear and fell down, as though they were dead. The angel said to the women, "Don't be afraid! I know you are looking for Jesus, who was nailed to a cross. He isn't here! God has raised him to life, just as Jesus said he would. Come, see the place where his body was lying."(CEV)

Careful note must be taken of the fact that the angel rolled away the stone from the mouth of the tomb, not to let Jesus out of the tomb, but as he said to allow Mary Magdalene and the other Mary to *"see the place where his body was lying."* This, of course, simply means Jesus was already out of the tomb when the angel rolled away the stone.

The mistaken assumption by many Christians reading this account is that the angel rolled away the stone to allow Jesus to get out. This, of course, is not the case as we've already demonstrated Jesus' ability to enter closed buildings without using a door. Jesus had already been resurrected from Saturday evening (the end of the Sabbath), and the angel's only purpose was to provide the visitor's with the evidence of this.

The Apostle Mark gives a similar account of the events, excerpted from the New Testament book of Mark 16:1-6:

"After the Sabbath, Mary Magdalene, Salome, and Mary the mother of James bought some spices to put on Jesus' body. Very early on Sunday morning, just as the sun was coming up, they went to the tomb. On their way, they were asking one another, "Who will roll the stone away from the entrance for us?" But when they looked, they saw that the stone had already been rolled away. And it was a huge stone! The women went into the tomb, and on the right side they saw a young man in a white robe sitting there. They were alarmed. The man said, "Don't be alarmed! You are looking for Jesus from Nazareth, who was nailed to a cross. God has raised him to life, and he isn't here. You can see the place where they put his body."(CEV)

In Mark's account, the visitor's to Jesus' tomb went out Saturday night (after the Sabbath) and bought spices to take to the tomb on Sunday morning. After arriving at the tomb they saw that the stone was already rolled away and an angel informed them that He was already resurrected. Again the angel pointed to the missing body as evidence that Jesus was resurrected.

Luke's account of the events differs only slightly. Luke account tells of two angels instead of the one mentioned in the prior accounts. Here is Luke's account excerpted from the New Testament book of Luke 24:1-8:

"Very early on Sunday morning the women went to the tomb, carrying the spices that they had prepared. When they found the stone rolled away from the entrance, they went in. But they did not find the body of the Lord Jesus, and they did not know what to think. Suddenly two men in shining white clothes stood beside them. The women were afraid and bowed to the ground. But the men said, "Why are you looking in the place of the dead for someone who is alive? Jesus isn't here! He has been raised from death. Remember that while he was still in Galilee, he told you, 'The Son of Man will be handed over to sinners who will nail him to a cross. But three days later he will rise to life.'"Then they remembered what Jesus had said."(CEV)

Again we see that Jesus was already resurrected before they arrived at the tomb. When they examined the tomb they discovered it empty and the angels informed them of His resurrection.

The final account is excerpted from the book of John 20:1-16:

"On Sunday morning while it was still dark, Mary Magdalene went to the tomb and saw that the stone had been rolled away from the entrance. She ran to Simon Peter and to Jesus' favorite disciple and said, "They have taken the Lord from the tomb! We don't know where they have put him." Peter and the other disciple started for the tomb. They ran side by side, until the other disciple ran faster than Peter and got there first. He bent over and saw the strips of linen cloth lying inside the tomb, but he did not go in. When Simon Peter got there, he went into the tomb and saw the strips of cloth. He also saw the piece of cloth that had been used to cover Jesus' face. It was rolled up and in a place by itself. The disciple who got there first then went into the tomb, and when he saw it, he believed. At that time Peter and the other disciple did not know that the Scriptures said Jesus would rise to life. So the two of them went back to the other disciples. Mary Magdalene stood crying outside the tomb. She was still weeping, when she stooped down and saw two angels inside. They were dressed in white and were sitting where Jesus' body had been. One was at the head and the other was at the foot. The angels asked Mary, "Why are you crying?" She answered, "They have taken away my Lord's body! I don't know where they have put him." As soon as Mary said this, she turned around and saw Jesus standing there. But she did not know who he was. Jesus asked her, "Why are you crying? Who are you looking for?" She thought he was the gardener and said, "Sir, if you have taken his body away, please tell me, so I can go and get him." Then Jesus said to her, "Mary!" She turned and said to him, "Rabboni." The Aramaic word "Rabboni" means "Teacher.""(CEV)

In all four accounts we've observed the following:

1. Those that went to visit Jesus went on a Sunday morning.

2. When they arrived the stone was already rolled away or was being rolled away.

3. The visitors to the tomb were all given the same message that Jesus was already resurrected.

4. The visitors to the tomb were all shown an empty tomb.

5. None of the visitors to the tomb witnessed the resurrection of Jesus but were all informed that He was already resurrected.

6. The stone was rolled away to provide proof to the visitors that Jesus was no longer there.

These four accounts of the resurrection of Jesus is further evidence that there could not have been a Sunday morning resurrection of Jesus from the grave. As stated before, Jesus was resurrected at the end of the Sabbath day.

"Resurrection Sunday," as it is called, is one of Easter's most important religious celebrations. The fact that it is a proven falsehood should be enough to convince the true Christian believer not to acknowledge or celebrate this event. Christianity is based on truth, the truth as outlined in the Holy Scriptures. "Resurrection Sunday" along with "Good Friday" are falsehoods and do not have their origins in the Holy Scriptures. Later in this book we will look closely into the Easter festival, its pagan origins, and why Christians should not celebrate it.

The Commission in the Four Gospels

The resurrection of Jesus from the dead began the true ministry of the Apostles. While Jesus came to die as Jehovah's sacrifice for the sins of all humanity, His secondary purpose was to prepare and commission His Apostles to spread this good news of the Gospel to all nations and all peoples. The establishing of the Christian church is outlined in the commission of Jesus to the Apostles in the books of Matthew, Mark, Luke, and John. The book of Matthew records the four basic instructions of Jesus regarding the establishing of the Christian church. These are summarized as follows:

1. The Apostles were instructed to preach the good news of the redemption of mankind from sin (the Gospel) in all nations of the earth.

2. They were to make disciples of those that were believers in all nations.

3. They were to baptize all believers in the name of the Father, and of the Son, and of the Holy Ghost.

4. They were to teach the believers to do everything Jesus had told them about the kingdom of God and salvation from sin through His blood.

Here is the actual text from the book of Matthew 28:19-20:

"Go to the people of all nations and make them my disciples. Baptize them in the name of the Father, the Son, and the Holy Spirit, and teach them to do everything I have told you. I will be with you always, even until the end of the world."(CEV)

We will take a more detailed look at this commission as we go forward. The commission, from the perspective of the Apostle Mark, is recorded in the book of Mark. He informs us that anyone who believes the Gospel and is baptized will be saved and that those that do not believe the Gospel of Jesus will be condemned. He also informs us that the believer will receive power from Jehovah, to do wonderful, miraculous things such as casting out demons and healing the sick. Below is the actual text from Mark 16:15-20:

"Then he told them: Go and preach the good news to everyone in the world. Anyone who believes me and is baptized will be saved. But anyone who refuses to believe me will be condemned. Everyone who believes me will be able to do wonderful things. By using my name they will force out demons, and they will speak new languages. They will handle snakes and will drink poison and not be hurt. They will also heal sick people by placing their hands on them. After the Lord Jesus had said these things to the disciples, he was taken back up to heaven where he sat down at the right side of God. Then the disciples left and preached everywhere. The Lord was with them, and the miracles they worked proved that their message was true."(CEV)

In his record of the commission, the Apostle Luke informs us in the book of Luke that repentance from sin and forgiveness of sin can come to the believer only through the name of Jesus and that the Holy Spirit would be sent to give power to the believers and the Church. Here is the actual text from Luke 24:44—51:

"Jesus said to them, "While I was still with you, I told you that everything written about me in the Law of Moses, the Books of the Prophets, and in the Psalms had to happen." Then he helped them understand the Scriptures. He told them: The Scriptures say that the Messiah must suffer, then three days later he will rise from death. They also say that all people of every nation must be told in my name to turn to God, in order to be forgiven. So beginning in Jerusalem, you must tell everything that has happened. I will send you the one my Father has promised, but you must stay in the city until you are given power from heaven. Jesus led his disciples out to Bethany, where he raised his hands and blessed them. As he was doing this, he left and was taken up to heaven."(CEV)

The book of John identifies Simon Peter as the leader of the newly formed church and he is instructed to feed followers of God. This part of the commission appointed Peter as the chief Apostle among the Apostles. Here is the actual text from the book of John:

"When Jesus and his disciples had finished eating, he asked, "Simon son of John, do you love me more than the others do?" Simon Peter answered, "Yes, Lord, you know I do!" "Then feed my lambs," Jesus said. Jesus asked a second time, "Simon son of John, do you love me?" Peter answered, "Yes, Lord, you know I love you!" "Then take care of my sheep," Jesus told him. Jesus asked a third time, "Simon son of John, do you love me?" Peter was hurt because Jesus had asked him three times if he loved him. So he told Jesus, "Lord, you know everything. You know I love you." Jesus replied, "Feed my sheep."(John 21:15-17 CEV)

It is certainly worthwhile to look very closely at the commission Jesus gave to the Apostles. The instructions contained here forms the very foundation of the Christian religion and the Christian church and serves as a guide to believers today in determining if we are still being obedient to the commission handed down to the Apostles from Jesus himself.

This is important for many reasons, chief of which is the fact that Jesus warned of those who would worship Him in vain. Before His crucifixion, Jesus warned about people who would worship Him but not as He had commanded them. In Matthew 15:9, Jesus said *"'It is useless for you to worship me, when you teach rules made up by humans.'"* *(CEV)*

It is for this reason that Jesus was so specific about His commission to the Apostles and why He commanded that the Apostles teach the new believers *"to do everything I have told you."* It is evident from the commission given the Apostles that doing what has been specified is as important as believing Jesus is the Messiah. From the commission we can determine that it was the responsibility of the Apostles and also for believers today to:

1. Be preachers and teachers in all nations and to all peoples.

2. Baptize the believer in water in the name of the Father, and of the Son, and of the Holy Ghost.

3. Teach that salvation from sin and the resulting consequence, eternal death, cannot be achieved through any other name but that of Jesus, the Son of God.

We will elaborate on each of these points to determine how much of the commission Jesus gave to the Apostles is being adhered to by churches today. Let us begin by taking a look at point number one, preaching and teaching the Gospel to all nations.

While it is a fair statement to say that the Gospel of Jesus is being preached throughout the world to all nations, to all peoples, and in all languages, it is also fair to state that much of what is being preached is not the word of God as Jesus instructed.

Today, satellites beam the Gospel throughout the world and it is a delightful experience to turn the television on at any hour of the night or day and see preachers and teachers of all ethnicities and cultures, speaking about Jesus, the power of the Holy Spirit, and inviting others to be saved from this world of sin, death, and destruction. It is truly wonderful and absolutely delightful.

This portion of the commission most certainly has been adhered to. What is of concern, however, is the preaching of falsehoods that have been incorporated into Christianity and are being preached and taught as the Gospel of Jesus. There are a number of very frightening instances that will be covered in this book. It is important to keep in mind that Jesus foretold of this and warned, *"It is useless for you to worship me, when you teach rules made up by humans."*

There are a number of glaring lies that are now being preached as a part of the Gospel. We have already covered the falsehood of the Friday crucifixion, which is celebrated, taught, and preached in most churches. We have also looked at the falsehood of the Sunday morning resurrection, which is celebrated, preached and taught as the day Jesus was resurrected from the dead. These two false teachings underlie, what has become one of Christendom's most celebrated periods, the period called Easter.

If the current teachings of a *"Good Friday"* crucifixion and a Sunday morning resurrection are falsehoods, then it safe to question the validity and truth of the whole business of Easter. Indeed, we will look at the origins of Easter to determine if it is from Christ and the

Apostles and whether Christians should be celebrating this festival. Another falsehood that will be exposed is the falsehood of Christmas.

Christmas and its pageantry, commercialism, and excesses have come to define the world of *"Christianity."* Nativity scenes are erected in churches along with decorated trees, lights, and a non-Christian character called Santa Claus. We will also look at the origins of Christmas and why Christian believers should not celebrate this festival.

Finally we'll look at the refusal of most Christians to observe the seventh day Sabbath in honor of Jehovah, and their insistence that Jesus authorized Sunday as the "new" Sabbath by His resurrection on Sunday morning. While there are many more falsehoods being preached in violation of the commission that Jesus gave his Apostles, we'll look closely at these three, Easter, Christmas, and Sunday as the Sabbath.

Easter

Let us begin by first stating that the celebration called Easter does not originate in Christianity. Easter is a pagan celebration that existed before the coming of Jesus, His crucifixion, and His resurrection. Surprised? Please don't be. The fact that *"Good Friday"* and *"Resurrection Sunday"* are both false should have been enough to lead us into questioning the validity of this celebration. Let us take a look at the customs of Easter and their origins. The festival of Easter has its origins in ancient pagan culture and worship and is tied to the celebration of fertility, the festival of the spring equinox, the rebirth of the sun god, and the celebration of the fertility goddess Ishtar (pronounced Easter). This is the reason Easter is celebrated with symbols such as the egg and the rabbit. These are all pagan symbols of fertility that were used in ancient pagan rituals dating as far back as the ancient kingdoms of Babylon and Assyria.

Here are some facts about the pagan goddess Ishtar:

1. She was the deification of the sex passion.

2. Her worship required the absence of sexual restraint and prostitution was a part of her worship in her sanctuaries.

3. Her temple priestesses were temple prostitutes who entertained male worshippers in sexual ceremonies.

4. She was represented as the creative force in all nature and the mother of all things.

5. She was responsible for the "renewal" of life that occurred each year around the time of spring, represented by the Easter egg and the Easter rabbit.

6. The Babylonians and Assyrians knew her as Ishtar.

7. In Palestine she was known as Astarte.

8. The Egyptians knew her as Isis and among other names the Greeks worshipped her as Aphrodite.

9. She is also known as the Queen of heaven and her worship is condemned in the Holy Scriptures.

10. Her husband was the pagan god Tammuz, the sun god, who dies each year in the summer and is reborn each year in spring.

11. There is weeping for Tammuz, led by Ishtar during the fall and winter months. As a result of his rebirth, fertility and joy returns to the earth each spring, hence the pagan spring festival called Easter, which is celebrated with fertility symbols such as eggs and rabbits.

12. The worship of Tammuz is also condemned in the Holy Scriptures.

The pagan origins of Easter are not in dispute by scholars and theologians. The sad truth is that most members of the clergy are all too aware of the origins of these celebrations, yet despite this knowledge they continue to proclaim this as a part of the Gospel of Jesus in violation of the commission to preach the true Gospel. The following scriptures, taken from the Old Testament books of Ezekiel and Jeremiah brings to our attention the fact that Easter predates the death, burial, and resurrection of Jesus. In Jeremiah 7:17-19 Jehovah describes the practice as an insult to Him as the people of Judah baked cakes to the Queen of heaven. Today these cakes are known as hot cross buns, an active part of the Easter celebration:

"Do you see what the people of Judah are doing in their towns and in the streets of Jerusalem? Children gather firewood, their fathers build fires, and their mothers mix dough to bake bread for the goddess they call the Queen of Heaven. They even offer wine sacrifices to other gods, just to insult me. But they are not only insulting me; they are also insulting themselves by doing these shameful things." (CEV)

Jeremiah 44:11-19 records God's punishment on the people of Judah for worshipping the Queen of heaven:

"I, the LORD All-Powerful, have decided to wipe you out with disasters. There were only a few of you left in Judah, and you decided to go to Egypt. But you will die such horrible deaths in war or from starvation, that people of other countries will use the name of Judah as a curse word. I punished Jerusalem with war, hunger, and disease, and that's how I will punish you. None of you will survive. You may hope to return to Judah someday, but only a very few of you will escape death and be able to go back. A large number of Jews from both northern and southern Egypt listened to me [Jeremiah] as I told them what the LORD had said. Most of the men in the crowd knew that their wives often burned incense to other gods. So they and their wives shouted: Jeremiah, what do we care if you speak in the LORD's name? We refuse to listen! We have promised to worship the goddess Astarte, the Queen of Heaven, and that is exactly what we are going to do. We will burn incense and offer sacrifices of wine to her, just as we, our ancestors, our kings, and our leaders did when we lived in Jerusalem and the other towns of Judah. We had plenty of food back then. We were well off, and nothing bad ever happened to us. But since the time we stopped burning incense and offering wine sacrifices to her, we have been dying from war and hunger. Then the women said, "When we lived in Judah, we worshiped the Queen of Heaven and offered sacrifices of wine and special loaves of bread shaped like her. Our husbands knew what we were doing, and they approved of it.""(CEV)

The book of Ezekiel 8:12-16 condemns the worship of Tammuz (weeping for Tammuz was a part of worship as they wept for his death in anticipation of his spring rebirth as the sun). His resurrection as the sun in spring involved bowing down to the rising sun and facing the east. It is also from this pagan practice that the tradition of Easter Sunday morning church services sprang. Jehovah clearly condemns these practices in this excerpted text:

"God said, "Ezekiel, do you see what horrible things Israel's leaders are doing in secret? They have filled their rooms with idols. And they say I can't see them, because they think I have already deserted Israel. But I will show you something even worse than this." He took me to the north gate of the temple, where I saw women mourning for the god Tammuz. God asked me, "Can you believe what these women are doing? But now I want to show you something worse." I was then led into the temple's inner courtyard, where I saw about twenty-five men standing near the entrance, between the porch and the altar. Their backs were to the LORD's temple, and they were bowing down to the rising sun."(CEV)

The Easter festival is a pagan festival that did not originate in Christianity and has nothing Christian about it. Easter is not a part of the Gospel of Jesus and never has been.

Christmas

The obvious pagan roots of Christmas are likewise without dispute. All Christians and non-Christians alike know that the celebration of a festival that purportedly hails the birth of Jesus and at the same time acknowledges the existence of flying reindeer pulling a sleigh from the north pole on Christmas Eve with a red-faced burly man named Santa Claus descending down every chimney and leaving gifts for both adults and children could not be authorized by Jehovah.

What is shocking is the fact that *"Christians"* lie to their children year after year in their attempt to convince them of the fabled existence of an all-knowing and all-judging Santa, who not only brings gifts but knows if they've been bad or good throughout the year. Churches, of all places, erect statues of this mythical Santa Claus, drape their buildings in lights and decorate the grounds of their sanctuaries with reindeer and sleigh alongside the nativity scenes depicting the birth of Jesus.

Shameless preachers openly admit that they know Jesus was not born on December 25, and they also openly admit that Christmas is not mentioned in the Bible, but find justification for the celebration using clichés such as *"putting the Christ back in Christmas."* If the spiritual consequences were not so serious the excuses would be laughable; however, given the seriousness of this form of idolatry, it cannot be treated as a laughing matter.

The pagan practice of erecting trees and decorating them with silver, gold, and other colorful ornaments as a part of worship continues in mainstream Christianity. The worship of trees is a pagan religious ritual. Has anyone every wondered why the gifts are placed under the trees? What does a decorated tree have to do with the birth of Jesus? Absolutely nothing! What do Santa Claus and his reindeer have to do with the birth of Jesus? You guessed it, nothing! Who is Santa Claus anyway!? Where did he come from? Where did Christmas come from since it is not in the Bible? These are just some of the questions we will be providing answers to as we explore the pagan roots of Christmas.

Where did Christmas come from? The festival called Christmas existed long before the birth of Jesus and therefore loses all credibility as a celebration of Jesus' birth. In fact Christmas is a celebration of a birthday, the birthday of the pagan God Saturn. To understand what Christmas is we need to go back to ancient times, back to the civilizations of Babylon, Assyria, and Egypt. We'll see in the Bible where Jehovah condemns the practice and then we'll go back to the

Roman Empire, look at the celebration there and the name change that took place.

In our discussion of Easter we spoke about the pagan goddess Ishtar (pronounced Easter), also known as the Queen of heaven and her husband Tammuz. Tammuz, the ancient Babylonian sun god was also known in other cultures as Mithra, Osiris, Horus, Adonis, and Saturn. In all these various cultures, his birthday was celebrated on December 25. In ancient Egypt Tammuz is known as Osiris and Ishtar his wife is known as Isis. Osiris and Isis had a son and named him Horus. Horus was also worshipped as the sun god. To the Greeks and Assyrians he is known as Adonis and to the Romans he is known as Saturn.

In all these cultures his death and rebirth has been celebrated for millennia. The celebration of his birthday has been commemorated on December 25 from ancient times. During the Roman Empire he was celebrated with a festival called Saturnalia which began on December 17 and lasted until December 25. The celebration was marked with drinking, giving of gifts, singing from door to door (under Christmas this became known as caroling), and licentiousness. The greeting during this festival was "Ho, praise to Saturn." Christmas is a reflection of what occurred during the festival of Saturnalia.

During the *"Christianization"* of the Roman Empire, the then Roman Catholic church sought to *"Christianize"* the pagan festival of Saturnalia by renaming it and adding Jesus to the celebration. Instead of "Ho, praise to Saturn," the greeting was changed to "Merry Christmas" and instead of "Saturnalia," the festival was renamed Christmas. Instead of the celebration of the birthday of Saturn, it became the birthday of Jesus. Everything else about the festival remained intact. It was still marked by drinking, revelry, exchanging of gifts, and licentiousness. Excepting for a name change, Christmas is still the festival that honors the pagan sun god Saturn.

Christianity is based on truth; the God of truth is Jehovah. It is a dishonor to Jehovah and His son Jesus to declare to honor Him in a festival built on lies. The analogy I've often used is that of a bottle of poison. If a bottle of poison is relabeled to read "Coca Cola" or "Pepsi," the new label will make it attractive to a person desiring a drink. The label change, however, does not change the content of the bottle. The poison still is poison, and poison kills.

The same is true for a festival created and dedicated to the pagan sun god. This was not a festival authorized by Jehovah or created by Him. It was created by pagan worshippers in honor of their pagan god. Changing the name of the festival and adding a lie that Jesus was born on this day does not sanitize this festival. Like the bottle of poison, the contents still kill. The celebration and worship of the sun god is condemned in the Holy Scriptures. We have already seen in our look at the pagan festival called Easter that the people of Israel were judged by Jehovah for their part in the worship of Tammuz. As we have already seen, Tammuz was known by various names throughout various cultures at various times in history. We've also seen that Tammuz is the same as Saturn. If Jehovah condemned the worship of Tammuz and his wife Ishtar (the Queen of heaven) in the books of Jeremiah and Ezekiel, will He then accept the worship of the same god because he has been repackaged and reintroduced under a different name and in a different festival? The scriptural response to this question is definite, Jehovah declares, *"For I, Jehovah, change not..." (ASV Malachi 3:6)* In the book of Hebrews in the New Testament it is written *"Jesus Christ never changes! He is the same yesterday, today, and forever."(CEV Hebrews 13:8)*

We'll now look at the Christmas tree and its origins. What we now call the Christmas tree has been around for millennia. From the time of ancient Egypt through to the Roman Empire, the tree has always been a part of ancient pagan worship. In Egypt the tree used was the palm and in pagan Rome it was the fir. In the Old Testament book of Jeremiah, Jehovah condemns the tradition of the tree and warns Israel not to adopt the customs of the pagans.

Here is the actual quote, taken from the book of Jeremiah 10:2-5, *"Thus saith Jehovah, Learn not the way of the nation...For the customs of the peoples are vanity; for one cutteth a tree out of the forest, the work of the hands of the workman with the axe. They deck it with silver and with gold; they fasten it with nails and with hammers, that it move not. They are like a palm-tree, of turned work, and speak not: they must needs be borne, because they cannot go. Be not afraid of them; for they cannot do evil, neither is it in them to do good." (ASV)*

The pagan origins of the Christmas tree are widely known; the fact that it has made its way into "Christian" homes and churches is in total disregard for the word of Jehovah. While many seek to justify the celebration of Christmas as the birthday of Jesus, how can the erecting of a decorated tree in the sanctuary of Jehovah be justified? What relation has this decorated tree with salvation, the birth of Jesus, or with anything Christian? Since these trees were the object of worship, why are they inside these sanctuaries and Christian homes?

In our Christian culture, the pagan worship of trees continues every year at Christmas time. Trees are revered, they are carefully decorated and strategically placed in public areas and in homes; gifts are placed under them so that homage is paid unto the tree in retrieving the gifts and songs are sung in honor of the tree. Without consciously acknowledging it, the modern Christian perpetuates the pagan worship of trees each year at Christmas time.

Santa Claus

Santa Claus has become a part of the Christmas tradition and has been endowed with various characteristic only attributed to Jehovah. Santa has been declared the following:

1. He is all knowing - He knows if children have been good or bad throughout the year and not only at Christmas. He knows all the children of the world by name and has an exhaustible list that tells their location on the earth.

2. He is present at all times - Santa can only know if children are good or bad only if he is with them all the time as an unseen deity.

3. He is all powerful - Only an all powerful deity could visit the billions of homes on the earth in a single night, sliding down chimneys, leaving gifts under a pagan tree, and flying away in a sleigh drawn by magical reindeer.

Christmas has made a god of Santa Claus. This should come as no surprise, however, as Christmas is the celebration that honors a pagan god, the ancient sun god that has been worshipped from the time of ancient Babylon. The sad irony of it all is that *Christian* churches have packaged Christmas as a part of the Gospel of Jesus and have unwittingly preached Santa as much as they have preached Jesus.

It is no mere coincidence that Santa is carefully packaged and fed to the minds of children. The Bible informs us that we should train children the way we would desire them to be and they will never turn away from the training. This is recorded in the book of Proverbs 22:6, *"Train up a child in the way he should go, And even when he is old he will not depart from it."(ASV)*

If the pagan practices are to be continued, then the minds of children must first be captivated by these celebrations. I remember that as a child, the worst thing that I believed could happen to anyone was for them to die before Christmas. In my mind not being able to celebrate Christmas was worse than death itself. I was very well trained and conditioned by society.

I was set free from this pagan form of worship when I accepted Jesus as my personal Lord and Savior and started reading the Holy Scriptures myself. The Scriptures declare *"'You will know the truth, and the truth will set you free.'"* *(CEV John 8:32)*

The commission given to the Apostles to preach the Gospel into the entire world has been perverted by the incorporating into the Gospel of Jesus, pagan traditions that corrupt the truth and make it a lie.

The Commission of Baptism & Making Disciples

As a part of the commission Jesus gave to His Apostles, they were to baptize those that believed and to teach them all that Jesus had taught the Apostles, thus making the new believer a disciple. Here is the previously quoted text, Matthew 28:19-20:

"Go to the people of all nations and make them my disciples. Baptize them in the name of the Father, the Son, and the Holy Spirit, and teach them to do everything I have told you. I will be with you always, even until the end of the world."(CEV)

This brings us to look closely at baptism and the prerequisites for baptism. The word "baptize" is derived from the Latin word "baptizare" and from the Greek word "baptizein", both of which mean "to immerse." From the etymology of the word we can conclude that to baptize someone in water is to immerse that individual completely in water. This complete immersion in water is demonstrated at the baptism of Jesus in the book of Matthew 3:16 when Jesus was baptized by John the Baptist, *"So Jesus was baptized. And as soon as he came out of the water, the sky opened, and he saw the Spirit of God coming down on him like a dove."(CEV)* Here we see that Jesus was actually in the water and the scripture records Him coming out of the water. The book of Romans 6:4 further describe baptism as a burial, *"Therefore we are buried with him by baptism into death..." (KJV)*

Burial indicates total immersion as one cannot be buried without being completely covered over. To immerse is to cover completely. We can therefore conclude that the practice of pouring water on the head of someone is not baptism as there is no immersion involved. This is very important in determining if the church is being obedient to the commission of baptism. This understanding of baptism allows us to state clearly the following:

1. The practice of pouring water upon the heads of babies and declaring them baptized is a falsehood that does not comply with the commission of baptism. These children have not been baptized.

2. The practice of pouring water upon the heads of adults, as was the case with Emperor Constantine while he lay on his death bed, is not baptism. Emperor Constantine was not baptized.

There are churches that engage in the practice of pouring water upon the heads of the believer, without the believer being immersed in water, and declaring them baptized. This is not in agreement with the Holy Scriptures. The purpose of baptism is to symbolize the death, burial, and resurrection of Jesus.

In the same way Jesus died by being crucified on a cross, the believer who accepts Jesus as Lord and Savior needs to die to this world and the desires of the flesh. The Holy Scriptures refers to this as crucifying the flesh. The crucifying of the flesh symbolically represents the death of that individual. Baptism is then the symbolic burial of that individual (the scriptures call this person "the old man") that will be no more. The coming out from under the water is symbolic resurrection of the new individual (the scriptures call this person "the new man"), who will no longer live after the desires of the flesh.

The Apostle Paul explains this symbolism in the New Testament book of Romans 6:3-4, *"Don't you know that all who share in Christ Jesus by being baptized also share in his death? When we were baptized, we died and were buried with Christ. We were baptized, so that we would live a new life, as Christ was raised to life by the glory of God the Father."(CEV)*

The other aspect of baptism that is worth examining is the name we should be baptized in. Jesus stated that the Apostles should baptize the believer *"in the name of the Father, the Son, and the Holy Spirit..."* An examination of the Holy Scriptures, however, reveals that they did not do this but instead went out baptizing believers in the name of Jesus. Was this disobedience to the commission or was it simply that the Apostles understood more of what Jesus was stating than many of us today do?

Many churches today baptize believers by stating the words *"in the name of the Father, the Son, and the Holy Spirit."* Let's say, for example, that a believer named John was being baptized, the pastor, priest, or bishop carrying out the baptism would state something like, "brother John, I now baptize you in the name of the Father, the Son and the Holy Spirit." They would then immerse John in the baptismal pool of water, river, or sea.

In the Holy Scriptures, however, we do not see this. The first baptisms done after the commission of baptism was given to the Apostles are recorded in the New Testament book of Acts. In Acts chapter 2, the Apostle Peter preached his first sermon and approximately three thousand people were made believers and were baptized. Here is an excerpt from this sermon as he extended the invitation for baptism to his listeners, *"Peter said, "Turn back to God! Be baptized in the name of Jesus Christ, so that your sins will be forgiven. Then you will be given the Holy Spirit."*

It is noteworthy that he tells them to be baptized in the name of *Jesus Christ* and not the *"name of the Father, the Son, and the Holy Spirit."* This repeats itself throughout the book of Acts and we see the early church performing baptisms in the name of Jesus.

Was this disobedience? Certainly not! We've already seen from the scriptures that Jesus is Jehovah, the creator of all things. This is why we are permitted to worship Him. The first commandment written by Jehovah in the Ten Commandments given to Moses on Mount Sinai commands the Israelites not to worship any other god but Jehovah. This is found in Exodus 20:3 *"Do not worship any god except me."(CEV)*

Because Jesus and Jehovah are one and the same, we are permitted to worship Jesus as we are still engaged in worshipping Jehovah and are not in violation of the first commandment. If Jesus were different from Jehovah, then worshipping Jesus would violate the first commandment of worshipping no other god but Jehovah. Jesus is the manifestation of Jehovah in human flesh. The scriptures also state that only the name of Jesus can bring salvation unto mankind and no other name. This is so because it was Jesus who died for the sins of mankind and no other person.

The book of Acts 4:12 inform us that *"Only Jesus has the power to save! His name is the only one in the entire world that can save anyone."(CEV)* We also know from the Holy Scriptures that Jehovah is the name of God. This is recorded in Exodus 6:3, *"And I appeared unto Abraham, unto Isaac, and unto Jacob, by the name of God Almighty, but by my name JEHOVAH was I not known to them."(KJV)*

Let us look again at the statement found in the commission Jesus gave the Apostles and substitute the names we now know into the commission: *"in the name of the Father, the Son, and the Holy Spirit"* would become *"in the name of JEHOVAH, JESUS, and the Holy Spirit."* The problem that arises here is that "Holy Spirit" is not a name and there is no name given the Holy Spirit in Scriptures besides that of God. "Holy" is an adjective that describes the "Spirit." To say Holy Spirit is the same as saying the "Spirit that is Holy" and that denotes Jehovah, the only "Holy" Spirit.

With this understanding, let us look again at the statement in the commission and substitute the names once more:

"In the name of the Father, the Son, and the Holy Spirit" is now rendered *"In the name of JEHOVAH, JESUS, and JEHOVAH."* Here we have meaningless repetition. Jesus' Apostles understood what many people today still find difficult to understand and accept and it is that Jesus, Jehovah, and the Holy Spirit are all one and the same. Jesus is the physical manifestation of Jehovah and Jehovah is a spirit, a spirit that is described as being holy.

This leaves us with only two names JEHOVAH and JESUS. Since it was Jesus who died (He being the physical manifestation of Jehovah as a spirit cannot be crucified and die), it is through His name only that anyone can be saved. This has been previously stated. The Apostles were therefore in compliance with the command of Jesus when they baptized believers only in the name of Jesus.

Churches should therefore be baptizing believers in the name of Jesus as this reflects a greater understanding of the commission Jesus gave regarding baptism. If however, baptism is being conducted in *"the name of the Father, the Son, and the Holy Spirit,"* no harm is being done. The commission is still being adhered to albeit with less of an understanding than the Apostles had.

66

Discipleship

With each baptism a disciple of Jesus is made. One responsibility that every baptized believer has is to communicate to others the good news of salvation. Salvation through Jesus cannot be a well kept secret. It is good news that must be shared so that others will be saved. This is how the Gospel of Jesus is spread throughout the world. Those who have received salvation become disciples of Jesus and in turn tell of their deliverance and share with others how they too might be saved.

The new believer in Jesus often faces a lot of challenges in their new found life and their new found faith. Friends, relatives, well wishers, and even antagonists all emerge as challenges to the new believer. The challenge is to communicate their faith to their fellowmen and women and to get them to understand that they need to communicate their faith because of love. This in itself is a challenge because there is the element of fear that comes with suddenly being different.

Often times the new believer is faced with ridicule and is ostracized. They often become the social outcast in their families and among former friends. They sometimes face hostilities and are sometimes cruelly treated. In some countries the threat of being killed for their faith is all too real. Yet despite all these challenges, the believer must tell the story of salvation to others as this is a part of the great commission Jesus gave to the Apostles.

Millions of people around the world face these hazards every day and continue to share their faith despite the risks of rejection and in some cases physical harm. Their faith is shared because love carries overwhelming power that can break down any barrier it faces. Many Christians are tauntingly asked the question, "What do I need to be saved from?" The answer to this question is why believers continue to tell the story of salvation to others at the risk of being rebuffed.

To appropriately answer this question, we first must understand the world we live in. To most people and to the scientific community, we live in a physical material world. We are taught in our schools that we are all animals and that we are made up of matter. There is no other world but what our five natural senses can interact with and when we die we cease to exist. This rendering of the world and of life itself would be very disturbing if it were true. It would take away all meaning to life and its purpose. We really would have no reason to live at all as we simply would be subjecting ourselves to a painful, empty, and meaningless existence. We would then die and cease to exist. This is the scientific view of life.

I need not dwell on how irrational and foolish this view is. Each person reading this book already understands that humans are more than flesh, blood and bone. We are more than just physical matter and the world is much more than we can see. The Holy Scriptures tell us of two worlds, the physical world that our senses interact with and the spiritual realm that our spiritual senses interact with. Yes, we all do have spiritual senses.

Before looking into the spiritual realm, we need to first redefine who we are as humans. We first need to reject the scientific definition of who we are. We are not animals; we are the crowning achievement of Jehovah's creation. We were created in the likeness of Jehovah, given an earthly body and a heavenly spirit. Yes, it is certainly true; we are all spirits living in a human body.

In describing what happens to humans at death, the book of Ecclesiastes 12:7, describes the returning to the earth of the physical body and a returning to Jehovah of the spirit that is truly the individual, *"And the dust goes back to the earth as it was, and the spirit goes back to God who gave it."(CEV)*

The truth is that our bodies are like clothing that we wear while we live on this physical planet; our seat of consciousness, the true us, which is our spirit, lives within this earthly robe. This is recorded in the book of Genesis 2:7 as Jehovah created the first human, *"And the LORD God formed man of the dust of the ground, and breathed into his nostrils the breath of life; and man became a living soul." (KJV)*

In this account of the creation of the first human, we see that the physical body of the first man was formed from the earth. He was not yet alive as the source of life was not yet placed into the body. The spirit was not yet into the body and the spirit is the source of life for the body. Without the spirit the body is just that, a body.

Jehovah then breathed into the body a part of Himself and it was then that the body became alive. The Holy Scriptures describe this event as man becoming a *"living soul."* A human being is composed of two entities, a physical entity and a spiritual entity. The body comes from the earth and contains no life in itself. The spirit comes from Jehovah, the source of all life, and therefore the spirit is alive.

The joining or fusing of the body and spirit together, an act that only Jehovah can accomplish, results in a living human or a living soul. It is for this reason that Jehovah states that human beings are created in His image. Our spirits came out from Jehovah and so we were like Him because we came out of Him. This is stated clearly in

Genesis 1:27, *"So God created man in his own image, in the image of God created he him; male and female created he them." (KJV)*

Human beings had the nature, personality, and character of Jehovah until we rebelled against Him in disobedience and took on the evil personality of Satan, the enemy of all that is good. This is the reason humanity is now plagued with cruelty, selfishness, hatred, murderous thoughts, licentiousness, homosexuality, adultery, child abuse, rape, and a host of abominations. The source of all this evil upon humanity is sin and the only solution available is salvation through Jesus, the son of Jehovah. This is what humanity needs to be saved from; sin and its natural and spiritual consequences.

The Spiritual Consequences of Sin

Sin carries with it both natural and spiritual consequences; however, we'll be looking closely at the spiritual consequences much more than at the natural consequences. The reason for this is that sin's natural consequences end with the death of the body or the physical person; the spiritual consequences, however, last for all eternity.

What are the spiritual consequences of death? To understand these consequences we take a close look at an actual event that Jesus describes in the New Testament book of Luke 16:19-29, *"There was once a rich man who wore expensive clothes and every day ate the best food. But a poor beggar named Lazarus was brought to the gate of the rich man's house. He was happy just to eat the scraps that fell from the rich man's table. His body was covered with sores, and dogs kept coming up to lick them. The poor man died, and angels took him to the place of honor next to Abraham. The rich man also died and was buried. He went to hell and was suffering terribly. When he looked up and saw Abraham far off and Lazarus at his side, he said to Abraham, "Have pity on me! Send Lazarus to dip his finger in water and touch my tongue. I'm suffering terribly in this fire." Abraham answered, "My friend, remember that while you lived, you had everything good, and Lazarus had everything bad. Now he is happy, and you are in pain. And besides, there is a deep ditch between us, and no one from either side can cross over." But the rich man said, "Abraham, then please send Lazarus to my father's home. Let him warn my five brothers, so they won't come to this horrible place." Abraham answered, "Your brothers can read what Moses and the prophets wrote. They should pay attention to that." Then the rich man said, "No, that's not enough! If only someone from the dead would go to them, they would listen and turn to God." So Abraham said, "If they won't pay attention to Moses and the prophets, they won't listen even to someone who comes back from the dead.""* (CEV)

After the physical death of the body (the separation of body and spirit), we do not cease to exist as the scientific community would like us to believe. As seen before, the physical body is buried in the earth because it came from the earth and the spirit, the true individual and the seat of consciousness, goes to Jehovah to receive judgment.

The book of Hebrews 9:27 state this very clearly, *"We die only once, and then we are judged."* (CEV) It is this judgment that determines our eternal destiny. If we had accepted the salvation offered through the sacrifice of Jesus Christ, had asked for and received forgiveness of our sins, had become a disciple of Jesus, living a life that reflected His righteousness through His mercies toward us, and kept Jehovah's commandments, then we would receive eternal life with Him.

We would be taken to a place called Paradise at the time of our death to be with Jesus and all the other believers that have also died.

If, however, we had not accepted the salvation that Jesus offered through His death, lived a selfish and self indulgent life, and did not observe the commandments of Jehovah, then a fiery place called hell is where we will exist for all eternity. This is called eternal death. This is what Jesus told of in the event excerpted from the book of Luke. It is not a tale but an actual event Jesus related.

Jesus spent much time while on earth, before his crucifixion, warning all about hell and describing the kind of place it is. While many foolishly comfort themselves with the falsehood that there is no hell and it only exists in the minds of those who believe it exists, the reality is far different.

Hell does exist and its existence is not dependent on the belief of humans. Below I've excerpted a number of quotes from the Holy Scriptures regarding hell and it existence. These are all quotes from Jesus himself:

"So if your hand causes you to sin, cut it off! You would be better off to go into life crippled than to have two hands and be thrown into the fires of hell that never go out" (CEV Mark 9:43)

"If your foot causes you to sin, chop it off. You would be better off to go into life lame than to have two feet and be thrown into hell." (CEV Mark 9:45)

"If your eye causes you to sin, get rid of it. You would be better off to go into God's kingdom with only one eye than to have two eyes and be thrown into hell. The worms there never die, and the fire never stops burning." (CEV Mark 9:47-48)

It is made clear in the Holy Scriptures that hell is a literal place. A place where fires burn forever and worms do not die. It is described in other areas of the scriptures as a place of great darkness and a place of untold suffering and unimaginable horrors. Hell is not just real, it is VERY real. This is the reason why new believers are so insistent in telling others of salvation through the death of Jesus. The zeal to share this information comes through the great love that the believer has for others and the desire to prevent another person from entering the horrible place called hell.

When an unsaved person asks "What do I need to be saved from?" the answer is very simple, the consequences of sin and a place called hell. The Holy Scriptures warns that *"Sin pays off with death. But God's gift is eternal life given by Jesus Christ our Lord." (CEV, Romans 6:23)*

The commission of discipleship is the commission that ensures the good news of salvation is spread to all peoples and nations on the earth. It is a commission that requires that believers be taught the truth of the Gospel, the truth of the commandments of Jehovah, and the truth of the spiritual consequences of sin. Sin holds the human family captive and only this truth can open the prison doors. Jesus said it best, *"You will know the truth, and the truth will set you free." (CEV John 8:32)*

The Weekly Sabbath Day

In our previous look at the death, burial, and resurrection of Jesus we also covered some aspects of the seventh day or weekly Sabbath day. Here we will look at Jehovah's commandment that all Christians worship on and keep the weekly Sabbath as a holy day. We'll also look at the origins of Sunday worship in Christendom and why it is in violation of the commandments of Jehovah.

The weekly Sabbath is first mentioned in the book of Genesis. Jehovah had completed all His work of creating the world in six literal days. It is important to point out that it was not six *"time periods"* as some have suggested but six literal twenty four hour days. To suggest six time periods as some have done is to imply that the Holy Scriptures is incorrect when it states six days. The reasoning around six time periods arises because faithless men and women with limited perspectives have decided that it is not possible for the world to have been created in six literal days and have therefore sought to equate Jehovah with their own limited abilities.

Since humans could not create so vast a universe in six days, they reason that the Holy Scriptures are mistaken as it must have taken billions of years. This is also the scientific viewpoint on the forming of the universe. Instead, they say, it has to be six undefined periods that are symbolically represented as days in the book of Genesis. This of course is not true as Jehovah did create the world in six literal week days. In response to these doubters Jehovah asks the question *"Is anything too hard for Jehovah?" (ASV, Genesis 18.14)*

After creating the earth in six days, the Holy Scriptures record that Jehovah rested on the seventh day, made it holy through His Divine declaration, and instituted it as a day of rest and worship for all humanity. At the time of the establishing of the weekly Sabbath, not a single Jew existed. This is important as there are many who incorrectly refer to the Sabbath as the *Jewish* Sabbath. There is no such thing as the *Jewish* Sabbath. The Sabbath was established for all mankind. Here is the text, excerpted from the book of Genesis 2:2-3, that records the establishing of the weekly Sabbath, *"And on the seventh day God came to the end of all his work; and on the seventh day he took his rest from all the work which he had done. And God gave his blessing to the seventh day and made it holy: because on that day he took his rest from all the work which he had made and done."(BBE)* Thus was the weekly Sabbath established, for all mankind and not Jews, at the end of Jehovah's creation.

The Ten Commandments given to Moses on Mount Sinai reminds us of the importance of the Sabbath day and our need to observe it and keep it holy. Because this was the only commandment that had been established at the creation, it is the only commandment that Jehovah wrote as a reminder. It is important to remember that Jehovah wrote the Ten Commandments Himself on two tablets of stone and then gave them to Moses. It is the fourth commandment of the ten and is written with a complete explanation of its importance.

Here is the text of the fourth commandment that reminds us to observe the weekly Sabbath; it is excerpted from the book of Exodus 20:8-20: *"Remember the sabbath day, to keep it holy. Six days shalt thou labour, and do all thy work: But the seventh day is the sabbath of the LORD thy God: in it thou shalt not do any work, thou, nor thy son, nor thy daughter, thy manservant, nor thy maidservant, nor thy cattle, nor thy stranger that is within thy gates: For in six days the LORD made heaven and earth, the sea, and all that in them is, and rested the seventh day: wherefore the LORD blessed the sabbath day, and hallowed it."(KJV)* Here are the salient points we'll extract from this commandment:

1. The Sabbath day is a holy day because Jehovah made it so. It is also a day of worship as it belongs to Jehovah and we are commanded to recognize its importance through worship.

2. We have been given six days to conduct our own affairs (work, school etc) but the seventh day, the Sabbath day, belongs to Jehovah.

3. Work is forbidden on this day for the entire family, even animals and including visitors to our homes.

4. The Sabbath day has been blessed by Jehovah above all other days.

During His sojourn on earth Jesus observed the Sabbath day and went to the synagogue to worship each Sabbath day. The book of Luke 4:16 describes this as Jesus' custom, *"And he came to Nazareth, where he had been brought up: and, as his custom was, he went into the synagogue on the sabbath day, and stood up for to read."(KJV)*

The Apostles also did the same while Jesus was with them and continued with the practice after Jesus' ascension to heaven. This is recorded throughout the New Testament. An example of this is found in the book of Acts 13:42-44, where we see not only the Jews coming together to hear the Apostle Paul preach the good news of the Gospel on the Sabbath day but also the Gentiles of the city of Antioch.

This was the day of worship and everyone went to the synagogue on the Sabbath day. Here is the excerpted text: *"And when the Jews were gone out of the synagogue, the Gentiles besought that these words might be preached to them the next sabbath. Now when the congregation was broken up, many of the Jews and religious proselytes followed Paul and Barnabas: who, speaking to them, persuaded them to continue in the grace of God. And the next sabbath day came almost the whole city together to hear the word of God."(KJV)*

Sunday morning worship and gathering for worship on Sunday's was not known to either the Apostles or to Jesus. It is not that Sunday morning worship did not exist. It certainly did. It was a practice of the pagans in honor of the sun god Saturn, as we have seen before. Saturn, as we have stated before, was known by many names throughout past civilizations and cultures and the practice of worshipping the rising sun on Sunday mornings has been done since ancient times. It was, however, unknown to the early Christians.

The explanation given by many church leaders that Jesus reestablished the Sabbath to be Sunday by his resurrection on Sunday morning has already been proven to be a falsehood. Jesus was not resurrected on a Sunday morning and therefore his resurrection did not usher in a new period of observing Sunday as the new Sabbath. Jesus himself declared that he came to change nothing but to fulfill all that was prophesied about Him and to die as the "Lamb of God" for the sins of mankind. He states this in the book of Matthew 5:17, *"Let there be no thought that I have come to put an end to the law or the prophets. I have not come for destruction, but to make complete."(BBE)*

He therefore then could not have come to put an end to the Sabbath day and its observance in honor of Jehovah, because He is Jehovah. He certainly could not change the Sabbath to Sunday in honor of the pagan sun god Saturn and there is no mention in the Holy Scriptures of any change as it relates to the Ten Commandments and the Sabbath day.

Since Sunday worship is not authorized by Jehovah, Jesus, or the Apostles, where did it come from and how did it become so much a part of Christendom?

Sunday worship has always been a pagan observance in honor of the sun god. Indeed, that is how the day received its name. Sunday is named in honor of the sun god. It is called the sun's day and has been around for millennia. The early church observed the Sabbath, ceased work on the Sabbath, and gathered for worship on the Sabbath. Like the early church, there are many believers who still do observe the Sabbath and gather for worship on this day. They cease all forms of labor from sunset on Friday and resume work only after the sun has set on Saturday evening.

In the book of Exodus 31:16-17, Jehovah tells Moses to inform Israel of the importance of observing and keeping the Sabbath holy, *"And the children of Israel are to keep the Sabbath holy, from generation to generation, by an eternal agreement. It is a sign between me and the children of Israel for ever; because in six days the Lord made heaven and earth, and on the seventh day he took his rest and had pleasure in it."(BBE)*

Of such importance was the observance of the Sabbath to Jehovah that the penalty in Israel for not observing it was death. This is recorded in the fifteenth verse of the same chapter in Exodus, *"Six days may work be done, but the seventh day is a Sabbath of complete rest, holy to the Lord; whoever does any work on the Sabbath day is to be put to death."* Of course, no one will be put to death today for not observing the Sabbath. Just as adultery, fornication, stealing, homosexuality, and a host of other transgressions do not carry the death penalty, violating the Sabbath day does not carry the death penalty. However, just as all the aforementioned acts are regarded as sin, so too is the violation of the Sabbath day regarded as sin in the eyes of Jehovah.

Sunday worship in Christendom was instituted not by divine order from Jehovah, but by the edict of a Roman Emperor named Constantine. Known as Constantine the Great, he was instrumental in making Christianity legal throughout the then Roman Empire and also launched the creation of the Roman Catholic Church.

Constantine was a worshipper of the sun god Mithra and in his attempt to unify Romans politically and spiritually he declared that

Sunday would be the day of worship and rest for all Romans. He was also anti-Semitic and wanted the Christians to have nothing in common with the Jews. Here is Constantine's edict issued March 7, 321 AD, *"Let all the judges and towns people, and the occupation of all trades rest ON THE VENERABLE DAY OF THE SUN: but let those who are situated in the country, freely and at full liberty attend to the business of agriculture: because it often happens that no other day is so fit for sowing corn and planting vines: lest, the critical moment let slip, men should lose the commodities granted by heaven."*

It can be argued that Emperor Constantine was the first Pope. He wore the title "Pontifex Maximus" which is the same title the Pope wears today and which is translated "Supreme Pontiff" in the English language. This was the title worn by the head of the College of Pontiffs, an ancient Roman pagan body whose members were the highest ranking priests in Rome's polytheistic state religion. It is clear that Constantine had no divine authority to change the day of worship from the Sabbath to Sunday, the day that honors the pagan sun god. Christians today who observe Sunday as the Sabbath pay homage to the sun god instead of Jehovah and acknowledge Constantine's authority over the divine authority of Jehovah and Jesus Christ, the son of Jehovah.

The role of the Apostles in establishing the early Christian church and their profound impact on the world is undeniable. The foundation of Christ's church was laid with the shedding of His blood on a cross so that the sins of mankind could be forgiven. The work of the Apostles ensured the foundation would not only remain but that the truth would be established forever. Though many false teachers, false churches, and false doctrines have sought to corrupt the true Gospel established by Jesus and the Apostles, they have not succeeded. The truth still cries out and falsehood is continually being exposed.

5

The Christian Doctrine:
Grace, Works, and Laws

The glory of the Christian religion lies in the fact that no one has to work for the salvation that comes through Jesus, they simply have to believe and embrace the free gift of Jesus' sacrifice. Throughout Christendom, the words Grace, Works, and Law are heard as often as Faith, Hope, and Love. In fact there is healthy debate in the Christian community regarding these three words. Many, however, engage in these discussions without first clearly laying out the definition of the terms and as a result arrive at no satisfactory conclusion.

It is indeed fair to state that because there is no clear definition agreed upon by so many, discussions regarding these words often create a sense of frustration to the believer who is in search of understanding. What is grace? Are we truly saved only by grace? Is there more required of us than just believing? What are works? Is keeping the Ten Commandments considered works? What are the Levitical Priesthood and the Law of Moses? Are the Ten Commandments a part of the Law of Moses? What Laws did Jesus' crucifixion bring to an end?

These are just a few of the questions that will be answered in this chapter as we explore from the Holy Scriptures what can be described as fundamental Christian doctrine.

Grace

We'll commence our discussion with a look at the Biblical definition of what grace is. The word grace first appears in the Holy Scriptures in the book of Genesis 6:7-8, and is used in relation to the prophet Noah. Here is the excerpted text:

*"And the LORD said, I will destroy man whom I have created from the face of the earth; both man, and beast, and the creeping thing, and the fowls of the air; for it repenteth me that I have made them. But Noah found **grace** in the eyes of the LORD."(KJV)*

Genesis chapter 6 records Jehovah's decision to destroy the inhabitants of the earth with a flood because of the gross wickedness that had so overtaken the lives of humans. Humans had become so corrupt, so evil, and so cruel that the only solution Jehovah saw was to bring an end to all of humanity. Noah, however, was different. He was not corrupt, cruel, or evil but was instead a fair man who walked in righteousness before Jehovah. The scriptures describe Noah as being a *"...just man and perfect in his generations..."* (*KJV Genesis 6:9*), and because of this he *"found grace"* in the eyes of God. What does this mean? This meant that, although all humanity was deserving of death by drowning, Jehovah's chosen method of punishment for the evils of mankind, Noah's uprightness would result in the species of humanity being spared total obliteration from the earth. Humanity was not deserving of being allowed to populate the earth and to benefit from the blessings of Jehovah; however, we were extended the privilege of living as a species through the righteousness of one man, allowed to repopulate and dominate the earth, and given the opportunity to walk before Jehovah in righteousness. In other words, we were given the privilege once more of *"getting it right."*

The story of the flood and Noah sums up the power of grace; it is favor that is extended to the undeserving. In the case of Noah, grace was extended to the human race because of the righteousness of one man. The salvation of all humanity through Jesus, the son of Jehovah, echoes the theme of grace recorded in the book of Genesis in the story of Noah and the flood. In the same way that humanity was spared extinction because of Noah's righteousness, it is in a similar manner that all humans who believe on Jesus will be spared extinction from natural and spiritual death.

Just as Noah's righteousness spared all humanity, the righteous blood of Jesus will save those that believe on Him from damnation and hell. Grace is the favor of Jehovah and cannot be bought, worked for, or earned in any way. It is given not because it is deserved but because Jehovah is merciful.

The Holy Scriptures informs us that we are saved by grace through faith and that it is the gift of God to all mankind. It further informs us that because our salvation was not worked for, no one is in a position to boast about their salvation; the New Testament book of Ephesians 2:8-9 states this very clearly, *"Because by grace you have salvation through faith; and that not of yourselves: it is given by God: Not by works, so that no man may take glory to himself."(BBE)*

Grace is a wonderful gift that Jehovah has given to us, a blotting out of our transgression against Him, and a washing away of all our sins without requiring us to pay the penalty for our evil deeds. We are all deserving of death but through the grace of God we will inherit eternal life as stated in the book of Romans, *"For the reward of sin is death; but what God freely gives is eternal life in Jesus Christ our Lord."(BBE Romans 6:23)*

The important point that must be taken note of is the fact that grace recognizes that sin does carry the penalty of death. Grace would be utterly useless if there were no consequences associated with sin. It is because sin carries such a terrible consequence that grace is greeted with such enthusiasm. It is this recognition of the consequences of sin that gives the gift of grace its potency.

There are many who fail to recognize this fact and therefore are less appreciative of the sacrifice that Jesus made on the cross. It must be stated clearly that grace does not eliminate the consequences of sin; the wages of sin is still death as stated in the scripture. Grace simply pardons the believer that is guilty of sin, granting the believer reprieve from the consequences because he or she has accepted the sacrifice of Jesus' blood. Jesus Christ is the gift of Jehovah to all mankind, the only gift that grants pardon to sinful mankind so that the sentence of spiritual and natural death is not carried out.

A gift, while given without compensation being required, is of no use unless it is received. This is the reason why the Gospel is preached in the entire world. While the gift of Jesus as a sacrifice has been freely given by Jehovah, there are many who cannot receive it as they are unaware that this gift exists. There are likewise those who will not receive it simply because they refuse to believe it is without cost. If a gift is not received, though it is freely given, it will not be of any benefit to those it is sent to.

For those who do not receive the gift of the sacrifice of Jesus, the son of Jehovah, the consequences of sin still hangs over them. This is the reason the Holy Scriptures state that we are saved by grace through faith. We can only receive the gift of Jesus Christ through faith, that is, we must believe that Jesus was sacrificed for us as a gift from God and that by receiving Him our sins are forgiven.

While the grace of Jehovah saves us from the consequences of sin, it must also be clearly stated that grace does not grant us a license to sin. There are many who confuse grace and the forgiveness of sin with freedom to disregard the laws of Jehovah. The Holy Scriptures gives us a definition of what sin is. Sin is not just anything we subjectively consider to be bad or unacceptable to us. Sin has a clear definition and it is outlined in the Holy Scriptures. Sin is the transgression or breaking of Jehovah's laws. Without Jehovah having given us a definition of sin, we would not know what sin is.

Humans are extremely subjective and what is considered righteousness in one part of the world is condemned in another part of the world. An example of this subjective nature of humans is seen in the practice of polygamy. While the Western cultures condemn polygamy as ungodly, many eastern cultures embrace the practice as righteous. This is just one example; there are many, many other examples of this subjective nature at work in the world.

Our views on what is sin and what is righteous are shaped by the cultures we are raised in and the traditions of those cultures. We would therefore be utterly confused on the subject of sin if Jehovah had not given us a clear definition. Culture and tradition do not define sin and cannot as they do not offer a universal objective definition. The book of I John 3:4 provide us with Jehovah's definition, *"Everyone who sins breaks God's law, because sin is the same as breaking God's law."*

Since sin can only be determined in terms of Jehovah's law, it is evident that grace does not eliminate the laws of God and subsequently grace does not eliminate sin. The function of grace is to eliminate the sins of the believer who accepts Jesus as Savior, and there is no requirement for compensation for those forgiven transgressions. The believer, who sins against Jehovah by breaking His laws even after being saved, continues to benefit from grace as long as he or she requests forgiveness.

It must be noted that forgiveness needs to be requested. This is stated in I John 1:9, *"If we confess our sins, he is faithful and just to forgive us our sins, and to cleanse us from all unrighteousness."(KJV)*

The grace of Jehovah will continually offer pardon for transgressions as long as it is sincerely requested. Grace does not permit us, however, to transgress Jehovah's laws at will. The Apostle Paul encountered this misunderstanding on the purpose and function of grace in the early churches. So pervasive was the misunderstanding that he dedicated several chapters of the book of Romans to clarifying the issue. In Christendom today, we have many who still have not understood the lessons the Apostle Paul sought to teach. It is because of this misunderstanding, and in some cases purposeful ignorance of what grace is, why churches today ordain practicing homosexual men and women to be bishops and priests and teach them that their sins are covered by the grace of Jehovah.

Grace is not license to live in sin; it is pardon for past sins and is available for future sins. This is entirely different from living a life of deliberate and purposeful sin. The Apostle Paul explains this clearly in the following verses excerpted from the book of Romans 6:1-7 and 11-15, *"What may we say, then? are we to go on in sin so that there may be more grace? In no way. How may we, who are dead to sin, be living in it any longer? Or are you without the knowledge that all we who had baptism into Christ Jesus, had baptism into his death? We have been placed with him among the dead through baptism into death: so that as Christ came again from the dead by the glory of the Father, we, in the same way, might be living in new life. For, if we have been made like him in his death, we will, in the same way, be like him in his coming to life again; Being conscious that our old man was put to death on the cross with him, so that the body of sin might be put away, and we might no longer be servants to sin. Because he who is dead is free from sin"*

"Even so see yourselves as dead to sin, but living to God in Christ Jesus. For this cause do not let sin be ruling in your body which is under the power of death, so that you give way to its desires; And do not give your bodies to sin as the instruments of wrongdoing, but give yourselves to God, as those who are living from the dead, and your bodies as instruments of righteousness to God. For sin may not have rule over you: because you are not under law, but under grace. What then? are we to go on in sin because we are not under law but under grace? Let it not be so." (BBE)

From this scripture it is evident that to benefit from the grace that Jehovah extends to us as a gift, we must be prepared to walk away from our previous lives of sin and walk in the newness of a righteous life in Jesus Christ. Since sin is the transgression of Jehovah's laws, to benefit from Jehovah's grace we must abide by these laws.

We are not under the rule of law. This must be understood, as the rule of law exacts penalties for breaking the laws. The believer that is saved by grace is under the rule of grace. Being under the rule of grace simply means that the transgressing of Jehovah's laws (which is sin), though punishable by death will be pardoned when the request for forgiveness is made. The consequences for breaking the laws of Jehovah are not imposed whenever pardon is requested. This is the power of grace.

Grace, however, did not eliminate the Ten Commandments or the various commandments of Jehovah found throughout the scriptures. Grace instead equipped us through our new spiritual birth to be able to resist our sinful impulses to transgress these commandments, hence the rhetorical question posed by the Apostle Paul, *"What then? are we to go on in sin because we are not under law but under grace? Let it not be so."*

Jehovah expects all who accept Jesus Christ as Savior to observe and keep His laws. These laws include His Sabbath day, which must be observed and kept holy. Many believers observe only nine of the Ten Commandments and then declare themselves to be under grace when it comes to the observance of the Sabbath day and keeping it holy. We have seen, however, that this declaration of being "under grace" so that license is taken in violating this commandment is a declaration made through ignorance.

Here is what the Apostle James wrote regarding the Ten Commandments, *"If you obey every law except one, you are still guilty of breaking them all. The same God who told us to be faithful in marriage also told us not to murder. So even if you are faithful in marriage, but murder someone, you still have broken God's Law."(CEV, James 2:10-11)*

If someone observes nine of the Ten Commandments and breaks one, that individual is guilty of breaking them all. There are additional commandments given by Jehovah that are not stated explicitly in the Ten Commandments. One such law is the commandment that forbids homosexuality. Though the Ten Commandments clearly state *"Thou shalt not commit adultery,"* it did not clearly forbid marriage between individuals of the same sex.

Adultery is defined as unfaithfulness in marriage and therefore those wanting to live in a homosexual relationship do argue that Jehovah does not forbid that kind of relationship as long as it is within the context of marriage. They argue that Jehovah condemns unfaithfulness but not a faithful relationship. However creative, this type of reasoning is twisted and erroneous.

The commandment regarding adultery was specific to marriage between men and women. Marriage was established by Jehovah at the creation when He stated, *"Therefore shall a man leave his father and his mother, and shall cleave unto his wife: and they shall be one flesh."(KJV, Genesis 2:24)* This was the first marriage, the joining together of the first man and the first woman in the Garden of Eden.

The purpose of the heterosexual marriage is to produce and raise children in a positive and productive environment; the emphasis being placed on the reproduction of oneself. This is the command that Jehovah gave to the first man and the first woman as recorded in the book of Genesis, *"God gave them his blessing and said: Have a lot of children! Fill the earth with people and bring it under your control. Rule over the fish in the ocean, the birds in the sky, and every animal on the earth."(CEV, Genesis 1:28)*

A homosexual relationship produces *NOTHING*. Two men or two women cannot reproduce themselves. It is a relationship that has its foundation in lust. It is sexual lasciviousness that requires that the flesh be satisfied despite the unfruitfulness of the relationship. It is for this reason that Jehovah condemns the homosexual relationship; it is in violation of his commandment to humans to multiply themselves and to fill the earth with people.

Throughout the Holy Scriptures, Jehovah issues commands against homosexuality, and the commands are very clear. In the book of Leviticus 18:22, Jehovah states, *"You may not have sex relations with men, as you do with women: it is a disgusting thing."(BBE)* He also condemns having sexual relations with animals, *"And you may not have sex relations with a beast, making yourself unclean with it; and a woman may not give herself to a beast: it is an unnatural act."(BBE, Leviticus 18:22)*

Jehovah found the practice of homosexuality so disgusting that the penalty for engaging in this kind of relationship was death under the Law of Moses. Here is the supporting text, *"And if a man has sex relations with a man, the two of them have done a disgusting thing: let them be put to death; their blood will be on them."(BBE, Leviticus 20:13)*

Male and female homosexual conduct is also condemned throughout the New Testament. In the book of Romans 1:24-28, the Apostles Paul writes regarding this, *"So God let these people go their own way. They did what they wanted to do, and their filthy thoughts made them do shameful things with their bodies. They gave up the truth about God for a lie, and they worshiped God's creation instead of God, who will be praised forever... God let them follow their own evil desires. Women no longer wanted to have sex in a natural way, and they did things with each other that were not natural. Men behaved in the same way. They stopped wanting to have sex with women and had strong desires for sex with other men. They did shameful things with each other, and what has happened to them is punishment for their foolish deeds. Since these people refused even to think about God, he let their useless minds rule over them. That's why they do all sorts of indecent things."(CEV)*

Indecent, disgusting, and evil are just some of the adjectives used to describe homosexuality throughout the Holy Scriptures. Clearly Jehovah is making the point that He is commanding us not to engage in such practices. Though the Ten Commandments do not contain the words "THOU SHALT NOT BE A HOMOSEXUAL," we see clearly that Jehovah has issued that commandment throughout the scriptures.

It is absolutely shocking to listen to ordained religious leaders on television and on the radio state that Jesus was silent on the issue of homosexual conduct and therefore they are not in a position to say whether or not it is sinful. I listened in absolute incredulity to an ordained minister of a major Christian denomination describe homosexuality as a gift that God had given to some people! It is no wonder so many homosexuals who are seeking to be delivered from this demonic practice are now believing that they can be saved without being changed, and also believe they will enter the kingdom of Jehovah as they are.

The scriptures are very clear on this point that HOMOSEXUALS will not be in the kingdom of Jehovah. Jehovah considers homosexual conduct disgusting. It is not from Jehovah, not approved of by Jehovah, and is in fact condemned by Jehovah. Jehovah considers it evil and reprobate and it is stated all throughout the Holy Scriptures. Here is what is stated in the book of I Corinthians 6:9-10, *"Don't you know that evil people won't have a share in the blessings of God's kingdom? Don't fool yourselves! No one who is immoral or worships idols or is unfaithful in marriage or is a pervert or behaves like a **homosexual** will share in God's kingdom." (CEV)*

The book of Isaiah 5:20 also warns anyone approving of this sinful lifestyle, *"Woe unto them that call evil good, and good evil; that put darkness for light, and light for darkness; that put bitter for sweet, and sweet for bitter!"(KJV)*

To state that homosexuality is a gift and that it is not clear from the Holy Scriptures that it is sinful is an attempt to deceive homosexuals that are seeking salvation into believing they don't have to change that part of their life as Jehovah already approves of it. This approach is the granting of license to sin and an attempted abuse of grace.

Being Born Again

No one can benefit from the grace of Jehovah unless they are born again, and the death of Jesus is of no benefit to an individual unless that individual is born again. Being born again marks the beginning of the sinner's journey back to Jehovah. It is the reason Jesus died and the foundational doctrine of the Christian church. It was the core of Jesus' message in the three and half years of His ministry on earth. Jesus first informed us that we needed to be *"born again"* in the New Testament book of John 3. The story is interesting; a Jewish Rabbi (teacher) was intrigued by Jesus' teachings and the miracles He did and wanted to speak with Him. Because the Jewish leadership at the time was hostile towards Jesus and His teachings, Nicodemus, as he was called, visited Jesus privately during the night time so no one would see him.

He began a conversation with Jesus by first stating that he believed Jesus to be a teacher sent from God. His reason for believing this was, as he stated *"... no man can do these miracles that thou doest, except God be with him."(KJV, John 3:2)* He had witnessed the miracles Jesus had performed, heard the teachings of Jesus and started to be in doubt about his own salvation. It can be reasonably argued that Nicodemus was driven to seek out Jesus by his fears that he was not truly saved. Jesus, knowing why he was there to see Him, seemingly brushed aside the compliment and informed Nicodemus that in order to be saved he must be born again.

There are many people today, some of whom will identify themselves as Christian, who are in the position that Nicodemus found himself in. Like Nicodemus, they are religious and attend religious services regularly, perhaps even once per week. They engage in religious discussions and are known in their churches or other places of worship, and people speak well of them. These characteristics are all identified in Nicodemus. He was an important man in Israel, a member of the ruling body called the Sanhedrin, the great council of seventy elders among the Jews, whose jurisdiction extended to all important affairs. They received appeals from inferior tribunals, and had power over life and death.

He was also a Pharisee, the strictest sect for religion and holiness among all Jewish sects and believed in the coming of the Messiah, all the writings of the Old Testament, the doctrines of angels and spirits, and the resurrection of the dead. He was also a teacher, as Jesus pointed out to him in their brief discourse, and historians have identified him as being extremely wealthy. Clearly Nicodemus was a man of great influence, wealth, and power in Israel. Despite all his importance, he was also a man in trouble. The kind of trouble he was in was not social, financial or political. He was in spiritual trouble, fearful about his eternal destiny and concerned about being saved. It was this spiritual need that he had for answers on how to be truly saved that Jesus responded to, not to his compliment.

Without verbalizing his question, Nicodemus was actually asking Jesus, *"How can I find the truth that will assure me that I'll be saved when I die?"* This is the question Jesus responded to when He said to Nicodemus, *"Except a man be born again, he cannot see the kingdom of God."(KJV, John 3:3)*

Here we see Jesus stating the most fundamental of Christian doctrines. A person who desires to be saved must be born again. There is absolutely no other way to be saved. Perplexed by Jesus' statement Nicodemus asked, *"How can a man be born when he is old? can he enter the second time into his mother's womb, and be born?"(KJV, John 3:4)*, to which Jesus responded, *"Except a man be born of water and of the Spirit, he cannot enter into the kingdom of God."(KJV, John 3:5)*

Jesus' statement is clear; being born again is an absolute essential, a prerequisite to being saved. A person may attend religious services, be a part of a sincere and dedicated religious family, perform good deeds, and be a respected member of society and still be lost to spend an eternity in hell. The prerequisite for salvation, as stated by Jesus, is being born again.

What did Jesus mean by *"born of water and of the Spirit?"* Since being born of water and of spirit is a prerequisite to entering into the kingdom of God, then we must seek to understand what this means. How does someone become *"born of water?"* To understand this we must take a second look at water baptism and its symbolic references. Earlier we saw that baptism is a symbolic representation of the death and burial of the *"old"* man, and the birth or resurrection of the *"new"* man. Here is the text again excerpted from Romans 6:3-4, *"Don't you* know that all who share in Christ Jesus by being baptized also share in his death? When we were baptized, we died and were buried with Christ. We were baptized, so that we would live a new life, as Christ was raised to life by the glory of God the Father."(CEV)

The definition of a literal birth describes *"the emergence of a new individual from the body of its parent."*(Merriam-Webster dictionary) In the same way a literal birth results in the emergence of a new individual from its parent, being born of water represents the emergence of a new, spiritual individual from the baptismal pool or from the waters of baptism. Jesus describes this as being born again simply because it represents a new spiritual birth.

It is evident that being immersed in water and then taken out does not result in any physical changes to the individual. What occurs, however, is a spiritual change; a change that cannot be witnessed with natural sight, but one that is experienced spiritually by the individual who has been baptized. To understand this change fully, it must be made clear that during natural child birth there is also spiritual child birth that takes place. Just as we have a biological father at birth we also have a spiritual father at birth. Two births occur at the same time, one that can be seen with the natural eye and one that can be only perceived and understood through a spiritual lens. We are given birth to naturally and we are also given birth to spiritually. We are born naturally to a biological father and we are also given birth to spiritually to a spiritual father.

Contrary to what many believe, we are not all the children of Jehovah at birth or even afterwards. The Holy Scriptures informs us that it is only those who receive Jesus that are given the power to become children of Jehovah. Here is the excerpted text, *"But as many as received him [Jesus], to them gave he power to become the sons of God, even to them that believe on his name: Which were born, not of blood, nor of the will of the flesh, nor of the will of man, but of God." (KJV, John 1:12-13)*

It is also stated in the New Testament book of Galatians, *"For ye are all the children of God by faith in Christ Jesus." (KJV, Galatians 3:26)* The scriptures also clearly state that we are all born in sin and there is no goodness in us. The prophet David (King David of Israel and author of most of the book of Psalms) in describing his spiritual state at birth, writes, *"Truly, I was formed in evil, and in sin did my mother give me birth" (BBE, Psalm 51:5),* and Jesus himself informed the Jews of His day that their father was not Jehovah but the devil. Here is the excerpted text, *"Jesus said unto them, If God were your Father, ye would love me: for I proceeded forth and came from God; neither came I of myself, but he sent me. Why do ye not understand my speech? even because ye cannot hear my word.* **Ye are of your father the devil,** *and the lusts of your father ye will do. He was a murderer from the beginning, and abode not in the truth, because there is no truth in him. When he speaketh a lie, he speaketh of his own: for he is a liar, and the father of it." (KJV, John 8:42-44)*

Below is the same text excerpted from the Bible in Basic English (BBE), which gives a clearer understanding of the text: *"Jesus said to them, If God was your Father you would have love for me, because it was from God I came and am here. I did not come of myself, but he sent me. Why are my words not clear to you? It is because your ears are shut to my teaching.* **You are the children of your father the Evil One** *and it is your pleasure to do his desires. From the first he was a taker of life; and he did not go in the true way because there is no true thing in him. When he says what is false, it is natural to him, for he is false and the father of what is false."*

As difficult as it is to accept, our cute little babies are not born spiritually to Jehovah but to his nemesis Satan. We were not born having Jehovah as our father either. Satan is the spiritual father of all humanity that stands outside the realm of being born again. This is the legacy of sin that was inherited from the fall of Adam and Eve, the fore parents of all humans. Their sin against Jehovah resulted in a rejection of Jehovah as their father and the adoption of Satan, the devil, as their spiritual father and that of all their descendants.

This explains why doing evil is natural and doing good requires effort, training, and guidance. It also explains why humans find pleasure in sinful acts such as fornication (sex outside the bond of marriage), homosexuality, adultery, stealing, and pornography. It also explains our tendency to rebel against authority and our desire to resist law and order. The history of the human race is adequately described as the history of war. Humanity is innately evil because our spiritual father is evil. Jesus describes him as a murderer from the beginning and also as a liar from the beginning.

Humanity exhibits the spiritual characteristics of Satan as he is the spiritual father of all humans that are not born again. We are not born the children of Jehovah; we become the children of Jehovah through Jesus Christ. Being born again results in a spiritual birth the Holy Scriptures describe as being *"born of God."* It is correctly summarized in saying that at the point of accepting Jesus as Savior and being baptized we "change fathers." The book of I John states, *"Whosoever believeth that Jesus is the Christ is born of God..." (KJV, 1 John 5:1)* The book of Mark also states, *"He that believeth and is baptized shall be saved; but he that believeth not shall be damned." (KJV, Mark 16:16)* From these two scriptures it is correct to conclude that to be *"born of God"* requires believing that Jesus is the Son of God and that water baptism is done after believing. One cannot be without the other. It is not enough simply to believe that Jesus is the son of Jehovah and then to consider oneself to be born again. The Holy scriptures also address this half measure. The book of James addresses those who were content with just believing that Jehovah is the only God and would stop there. The Apostles James writes to them and informs them that even demons believe this, so there is not much accomplished if they were to stop simply at believing. Here is the text, *"You surely believe there is only one God. That's fine. Even demons believe this, and it makes them shake with fear."(CEV, James 2:19)* It is for this reason that the scriptures state that belief that Jesus is the son of Jehovah must be accompanied with baptism. Without baptism there is no new birth. Being born again only occurs through baptism. It is at the point of baptism that we become adopted children of Jehovah; we cast off and sever our spiritual relationship with Satan, embrace Jesus as our Savior and brother, and receive the embrace of Jehovah as his children.

We are then born again. We become sons and daughters of Jehovah and are now being led by His Holy Spirit as recorded in the book of Romans, *"For as many as are led by the Spirit of God, they are the sons of God. For ye have not received the spirit of bondage again to fear; but ye have received the Spirit of adoption, whereby we cry, Abba, Father. The Spirit itself beareth witness with our spirit,* **that we are the children of God**" *(KJV, Romans 8:14-16)*

We are now clear on what it means to be born of water. We'll now look at what it means to be born of *"the Spirit."* To understand the concept of being born of the Spirit, it is necessary to look at our earlier discussion about the composition of the human being. We had seen earlier that a person is a composite of a physical body and a spirit that was given by Jehovah. Thus we saw in the book of Genesis that the body of man was taken from the earth, and it was lifeless. Jehovah blew a part of Himself into the lifeless body and the body came alive. Man then was described as a living soul. From this and other scriptures we've seen that a person is not his or her body. The body is like a garment that covers or houses the true person, the spirit that exists within the body. We've also seen from the scriptures, that at the time of death, the spirit separates from the body and goes back to Jehovah to receive judgment for the life lived while in the body.

At the time of natural birth we are all born with a spirit, the true us, that lives inside our bodies. This spirit is not innately good or righteous and as we grow up our spirit begins to manifest its desires which for the most part tend to be evil, rebellious and ungodly. This is the reason children must be scolded and corrected as the scriptures warn *". . . a child who is not guided is a cause of shame to his mother."* *(BBE 29:15)*

Our spirits are not righteous because of the spiritually inherited sins from our parents and fore parents, going back to the sins of Adam and Eve. Since we are born naturally with unrighteous spirits, being born again requires that we also receive a new or renewed spirit from Jehovah. This is what Jesus meant by being born of *"the Spirit."* Please take careful note that Jesus did not say we must be born of *"a"* spirit but of *"the"* spirit. This is important as the scriptures state that there are many spirits in the world that are not of God or from God. Here is the Apostle John's warning to the brethren of the church, *"My loved ones, do not put your faith in every spirit, but put them to the test, to see if they are from God. . ."* *(BBE, 1 John 4:1)*

To be born of *"the"* Spirit is a reference to being born of the Holy Spirit of Jehovah, to have the evil spirit we were born with renewed in the Holy Spirit of Jehovah. It is only through this renewal of our spirits by the Holy Spirit that we are able to have righteous thoughts and subsequently be able to do righteous acts. Our spirits are born again by being cleansed by the Holy Spirit. This is explained in the book of Titus, *"God washed us by the power of the Holy Spirit. He gave us new birth and a fresh beginning. God sent Jesus Christ our Savior to give us his Spirit."* (CEV, Titus 3:5-6)

This is the same as saying that our spirits are regenerated by the Holy Spirit, we experience a profound change in our spirits that brings great positive changes that begin to be manifested in our bodies. Our spirits are reformed to desire the things of Jehovah, righteousness begins to appeal to us, and sin suddenly becomes repulsive.

This explains the sudden change in desire that occurs in many individuals immediately after being born again. I recall vividly the testimony of a former cocaine addict who gave his life to Jesus and experienced the sudden cleansing of his spirit and an instant loathing of cocaine. Without checking into rehab he was instantly purged of his desire of the drug and of his addiction. There is also the testimony of the addict to pornography who almost vomited when he saw pornographic photographs he formerly had great delight in. There are thousands of such testimonies in every culture, on every continent, and in every race; people who are born of the Spirit, the Holy Spirit, and experience the cleansing and purifying of their spirits by the Holy Spirit of Jehovah.

Without this rebirth in spirit, Jesus declares that we cannot enter the kingdom of Jehovah. Transformation of perspective, of thought, of desires occurs when one's spirit is born of Jehovah's Holy Spirit. This is described throughout the Holy Scripture as being renewed in mind. This is not a change that is imposed on oneself through discipline and struggle with the flesh. This is a spiritual change in appetite that rejects the things that are ungodly and a new found desire for the things of Jehovah.

This change in desires occurred in the case of the Apostle Paul, who persecuted the church and approved of the death of the saints prior to being born again, but was willing to give his life for the Gospel of Jesus immediately after being transformed in spirit. In the book of Romans he advises us to be similarly transformed to the point of giving our lives as a living sacrifice to Jehovah. In other words we live no longer for ourselves, our desires, or our satisfaction but instead for Jesus Christ our Lord and Savior. Here is the Apostle Paul's urging, *"I beseech you therefore, brethren, by the mercies of God, that ye present your bodies a living sacrifice, holy, acceptable unto God, which is your reasonable service. And be not conformed to this world: but be ye transformed by the renewing of your mind, that ye may prove what is that good, and acceptable, and perfect, will of God."(KJV, Romans 12:1-2)*

Works of the Law & the Levitical Priesthood

Throughout the New Testament, and particularly the books written by the Apostle Paul, there is continuous mention of the law, the works of the law, and the Levitical Priesthood. The books of Romans, Galatians, Ephesians, and Hebrews engage the reader in lengthy discussions on these topics. The book of Hebrews details much information about the Levitical Priesthood, Galatians and Ephesians details information on the law and its purposes, and the book of Romans addresses matters relating to Jews and Gentiles regarding the law and salvation.

Despite the Apostle Paul's lengthy discussions on these topics there are still many Christians who have failed to understand the purpose of Paul's discussions. There are those who do not understand what law the Apostle Paul was speaking about, why so much attention was focused on the law, and what the Levitical Priesthood was.

Failure to understand these issues will undoubtedly lead readers of the New Testament books to incorrect conclusions that are not intended by the Holy Scriptures. It is for this reason that we'll be looking at this very important topic of the law as spoken of in the New Testament books of the Bible.

There are many Christians who declare that they are *"New Testament"* Christians, that is, they only read the New Testament and regard the Old Testament as having no spiritual relevance. They make mention of the Old Testament only in a historical context and dismiss its spiritual virtues and relevance to the salvation of the believer. This approach to the Holy Scriptures is not only wrong, it can only be described as folly. It must be clearly stated that without knowledge of the Old Testament, there can be no understanding or appreciation of the New Testament. It must also be pointed out that the Apostles of Jesus and Jesus Himself had only the Old Testament as their guide and as the only source of spiritual reference.

The book we embrace today as the New Testament did not exist during the times of the Apostles, as it is a compilation of their letters to various churches over the length of their various ministries. It is my opinion that Christians who ignore the Old Testament in preference of declaring that they are *"New Testament Christians"* only, place themselves in great spiritual peril.

Let us look carefully at the word testament and its various meanings. The word "testament" has several meanings; the most common use is that of an agreement with God or a covenant with God. It also means a *"will"* as in someone's last will and testament and finally it also means *"witness"* as in someone who provides material evidence. From our understanding of the word *"testament,"* The Old Testament then is Jehovah's former or *"Old"* covenant with humanity while the New Testament is His current or *"New"* covenant with humanity.

The Apostle Paul also uses testament to mean "will," as in last will and testament, during his discussion of the law and the death of Jesus in the book of Hebrews. He makes reference to Jesus as a testator, that is the person who makes a will, and to the *"New"* covenant as being that will. He explains that while the testator is alive the will has no power as a will can only be executed upon the death of the testator. Jesus then, he explains is the testator, the author of the New Testament, which became effective at the time of His death on the cross. Here is the excerpted text, *"Because where there is a testament, there has to be the death of the man who made it. For a testament has effect after death; for what power has it while the man who made it is living?" (BBE, Hebrews 9:16-17)*

The Old Testament or old covenant is therefore extremely relevant in a spiritual and historical sense if there is to be appreciation and understanding of the New Testament or new covenant. It cannot be dismissed or put aside and simply declared *"nailed to the cross of Jesus,"* as some will say. The fact is that the new covenant was given birth to out of the old and was not *"nailed to the cross,"* but fulfilled. This is an extremely important point as this understanding of the fulfillment of the old covenant will shed a great light on our understanding of the new covenant established through the death of Jesus.

To comprehend much of what the Apostle Paul wrote regarding the law we must go back to the Old Testament so that we can understand his writings. Paul was a scholar of the Old Testament and describes himself as being a Jew, who was educated in the law by Gamaliel, an esteemed member of the Sanhedrin (the council of seventy elders that ruled Israel) and a great scholar of the law.

Paul was also descended from the tribe of Benjamin and belonged to the Jewish sect called the Pharisees. In the following excerpted verses the Apostle Paul tells us briefly about himself, *"I am a Jew of Tarsus in Cilicia by birth, but I had my education in this town [Jerusalem] at the feet of Gamaliel, being trained in the keeping of every detail of the law of our fathers; given up to the cause of God with all my heart..."(BBE, Acts 22:3) "...if any other man has reason to have faith in the flesh, I have more: Being given circumcision on the eighth day, of the nation of Israel, of the tribe of Benjamin, a Hebrew of Hebrews; in relation to the law, a Pharisee" (BBE, Philippians 3:4-5)*

The reason the Apostle Paul details his credential in the scriptures, is not to boast as he points out, but to establish his legitimacy in addressing issues regarding the law. The writings of the Apostle Paul will be our authoritative source in discussing matters of the law in the New Testament. In addition to the writings of Paul, there is another important distinction that must be made before we wade into this discussion and that is the difference between the Law of Moses and the law of the Ten Commandments.

It was previously pointed out that the law of the Ten Commandments was originally written by the finger of Jehovah on two tables or tablets of stone that were then handed to Moses by Jehovah. This is recorded in the book of Exodus, *"And when his [Jehovah] talk with Moses on Mount Sinai was ended, he gave him the two stones of the law, two stones on which was the writing made by the finger of God."(BBE, Exodus 31:18)*

The laws that became known as the Law of Moses are also described throughout the scriptures as the added laws, the laws of ordinances, the laws of the Levitical Priesthood, and also the book of the law. These were given to Moses afterward and were written by Moses in a book. These laws were largely ceremonial; they outlined rituals that had to be carried out during worship, rules on sacrifices to be offered, various washings to be done before appearing before Jehovah for worship, laws governing sexual relationship, and many more rules relating to atonement for sin. The law also detailed various feasts that had to be observed, when they were to be celebrated, and how they were to be celebrated. The law of circumcision, the requirement that all male children had to be circumcised eight days after birth was also a part of this book. It also contained information about all the other Sabbaths, in addition to the weekly Sabbath. These ordinances and rituals are referred to throughout the New Testament as the works of the law, that is to say, activities that the Israelites had to engage in under the Old Testament or old covenant to ensure their salvation.

The Apostle Paul's writings on the subject of the law cannot be understood if the distinction between the Law of Moses and the law of the Ten Commandments is not made. The Old Testament or old covenant was established through the sacrificial blood of animals as a binding agreement between Jehovah and Israel. The Law of the Ten Commandment was not. It existed before the establishing of this covenant. It existed from the time of the creation.

The Old Testament or old covenant was not between Jehovah and the rest of the world but strictly between Jehovah and Israel. In contrast, the Law of the Ten Commandment is a universal law that is binding to all mankind. The establishing of the Old Testament or old covenant is recorded in the following verses excerpted from the book of Exodus:

*"Then Moses came and put before the people all the words of the Lord and his laws: and all the people, answering with one voice, said, Whatever the Lord has said we will do. Then **Moses put down in writing all the words of the Lord**, and he got up early in the morning and made an altar at the foot of the mountain, with twelve pillars for the twelve tribes of Israel. And he sent some of the young men of the children of Israel to make burned offerings and peace-offerings of oxen to the Lord. And Moses took half the blood and put it in basins; draining out half of the blood over the altar. And he **took the book of the agreement**, reading it in the hearing of the people: and they said, Everything which the Lord has said we will do, and we will keep his laws. Then Moses took the blood and let it come on the people, and said, This blood is the sign of the agreement which the Lord has made with you in these words."(BBE, Exodus 24:3-8)*

The book of the agreement that is mentioned in these excerpted verses contained the laws written down by Moses as he received them from Jehovah. These are the Law of Moses and the covenant regarding these laws was strictly confined to Jehovah and the Israelites. The following important points summarize the distinction between the Law of Moses and the law of the Ten Commandments:

1. The Ten Commandments were written on tables of stone by Jehovah and given to Moses.

2. The Law of Moses was spoken by Jehovah and written down by Moses in a book described as the book of the law.

3. The Ten Commandments were spoken by Jehovah directly to the people of Israel from Mount Sinai (This is recorded in Exodus 20:1-17)

4. The Law of Moses was read to the people by Moses.

5. The Ten Commandments are universal laws that apply to all humanity (*Murder was forbidden from the beginning of creation, the weekly Sabbath was established on the seventh day, stealing was forbidden etc*)

6. The Law of Moses was only applicable to the Israelites as a part of the old covenant.

7. The Ten Commandments are eternal laws that will govern the earth forever.

8. The Law of Moses was temporary until the coming of Jesus Christ.

We'll now look at the Levitical priesthood. An understanding of the Law of Moses allows us to understand the Levitical priesthood as one is dependent on the other for relevance. It is also important to understand the Levitical priesthood so that we can understand why it is no longer necessary and we can truly appreciate why the Holy Scriptures refer to Jesus as our High Priest. We'll delve more deeply into Jesus being our High Priest later on in this chapter.

The Levitical priesthood was instituted by Jehovah after the Israelites were delivered by Him from slavery in Egypt. Jehovah selected Moses' brother Aaron and his sons to be priests before him. This is recorded in the Old Testament book of Exodus as Jehovah spoke with Moses, "*Send for your brother Aaron and his sons Nadab, Abihu,*

Eleazar, and Ithamar. They are the ones I have chosen from Israel to serve as my priests."(CEV, Exodus 28:1)

Aaron was from the Israelite tribe of Levi and only members of this tribe would be permitted to be priests by Jehovah. The term "Levitical" is derived from the word "Levi" and denotes the priestly tribe of Israel. Thus we have the Levitical Priesthood, the priesthood in Israel before the sacrifice of Jesus and the establishing of the New Testament or new covenant with Jehovah. Under the Old Testament or covenant with Jehovah, the priests played a very important role. They were the ones authorized by Jehovah to appear before Him on behalf of the people of Israel. They offered the various sacrifices to Jehovah on behalf of the people and were consecrated to minister before Jehovah for all their lives.

The role of the priest was of particular importance especially as it related to the sins of the people. Atonement for sin had to be made by a sacrifice called a sin offering. This sacrifice was to be a bull that the priest and only the priest had to sacrifice before Jehovah. The shedding of the blood of this animal was to atone for the sins of the people. This had to be done every year; there was no other way to atone for the nations sins. Access to Jehovah came only through the priests and since the priests were of the tribe of Levi, then it meant that access to Jehovah came through the tribe of Levi. This seemingly insignificant fact is actually very important in comprehending the differences between the old and new covenants.

To indicate the end of the old covenant, Jehovah sent Jesus, not through the lineage of Levi, but through the lineage of Judah. Jesus descended from the tribe of Judah, a tribe from which it was not permitted that there should be a priest under the old covenant. Jesus, however, is described in the New Testament as the High Priest of the believer and this shifting of the priestly tribe signaled a move from the old covenant to the new. Access to Jehovah is still through the priesthood; however, it is now through the priesthood of Jesus and the tribe of Judah and no longer through the Levitical priesthood.

This effectively brought about the fulfillment of the prophecy recorded in the Old Testament book of Jeremiah 31:31 with regards to the new covenant, *"See, the days are coming, says the Lord, when I will make a new agreement with the people of Israel and with the people of Judah"* (BBE, *Jeremiah 31:31*)

This shifting of the priesthood from the Levites to Jesus along with Jesus' ultimate sacrifice as the Lamb of God did not destroy the old covenant, as some say, it simply fulfilled it. The old covenant was brought to its completion; the sacrifices, washings, ordinances, and rituals that were recorded by Moses in the book of the law were now satisfied by one sacrifice, Jesus, the son of Jehovah.

The Apostle Paul writes about the fulfillment of the Law of Moses in the book of Galatians, *"What then is the law? It was an addition made because of sin, till the coming of the seed to whom the undertaking had been given..."* (BBE, *Galatians 3:19*) Note that Paul describes the law as an addition that was necessary until the coming of Jesus (the seed). If the law was an addition it had to be added to something that existed prior to it.

Since we know that the law of the Ten Commandment existed since the time of creation and that sin is defined as the transgressing of the Ten Commandments law, we know from these two facts that the Law of Moses were given specifically to provide a remedy for the breaking of the Ten Commandments. The Law of Moses was provided as the means through which the people of Israel could atone for their sins until the fulfillment of the coming of Jesus, who would be the permanent atonement for sin, thus establishing the need for the Levitical priesthood. The Levitical priesthood would exist for as long as the Law of Moses was binding.

Jesus' sacrifice effectively replaced the Law of Moses, fulfilled the prophecies regarding the new covenant, and removed the need for additional law to the Ten Commandments. Thus the Apostle Paul describes the Law of Moses as a school master whose job it was to instruct the Israelites until the coming of Jesus, *"Wherefore the law was our schoolmaster to bring us unto Christ, that we might be justified by faith."(KJV, Galatians 3:24)*

Born again believers in Jesus, who declare that they are no longer under the law and therefore have no need to observe the Ten Commandments, exhibit their ignorance of the old and new covenants. It is highly probable that they have no understanding of the Old Testament or the New Testament and genuinely need to be instructed in why there are two testaments. It is also true that there are many people who are aware of the truth and choose simply to ignore it while there are others who are being misled by members of the clergy who are themselves blind to the truth.

The following is a true story; it is an account of an experience I had a few years ago with a new convert to the Christian religion. The story highlights the need for an understanding of the old and new covenants in the churches and also for obedient men and women in ministry. A few years ago I was introduced to a young woman; she had recently been baptized and had accepted Jesus as her Lord and personal Savior. She had been given the right hand of fellowship (that is to say she was given membership in the church she was baptized in), and was a born again believer. She happily relayed to me her spiritual experiences and her journey to becoming a Christian.

I was very happy for her and we spoke enthusiastically about Jehovah, Jesus, the Holy Spirit, and many other spiritual things. We exchanged telephone numbers and parted company. Though she knew I was a Sabbath keeper and a keen observer of the Ten Commandments (this came out in our discussion), our discussions were not focused on our differences but on our joy in being saved.

Several months passed after that initial meeting. I received a phone call late one Friday evening from her and needless to say I was very excited to hear from her again. Her call was troubling and I knew something was wrong. She would not discuss the details on the phone so we set a date to meet the following week so we could discuss her cause for concern. It was at this meeting that she relayed to me the most astonishing story. She informed me that shortly after our meeting, she had received the baptism with the Holy Spirit (we'll discuss this baptism later on), and immediately thereafter the Holy Spirit in her began to inform her that she was transgressing the commandments of Jehovah.

Perplexed by this message she sought for an answer through prayer and fasting and it was then told to her by the Spirit of Jehovah (the Holy Spirit) that she was not observing the Sabbath day. In her quest to find out if she was the only person having this experience, she started relaying her experiences to her fellow church members. Their responses surprised her! She discovered she was not the only person having the experience. A senior member of her church then informed her that the same thing happened to him a few years after he was baptized with the Holy Spirit and advised her to ignore the voice and it will eventually go away. He informed her that he had done exactly that and the voice ceased to speak to him further about the Sabbath.

She could not believe all she was being told and in her search for answers frantically called me. I spent the next few months teaching her about the Ten Commandments, the Holy Sabbath Day, the old covenant, and the new covenant. I urged her to speak to her pastor about her discoveries and receive from him clarification about the Ten Commandments and the Sabbath Day. She returned a few weeks later completely disheartened but with a made up mind to leave her church. She informed me that her pastor already knew and could not offer her an explanation as to why he had not led the church in the direction outlined by Jehovah.

Today the young woman of the story is a Sabbath keeper, an observer of the Ten Commandments, and a happy born again believer. I arrived at the conclusion that these believers in Jesus were disobedient to the voice of the Holy Spirit because they confused the Ten Commandments with the Law of Moses and considered them to be one and the same. Since the Law of Moses was fulfilled, they resisted the voice of the Holy Spirit that informed them that they should be keepers of the weekly Sabbath. Ignorance of truth will lead ultimately to disobedience to Jehovah.

The pastor in this story knew the members of his congregation were being informed by the Holy Spirit to observe the Ten Commandments but chose to be disobedient (I believe through ignorance).

It is a sad fact that a large number of those making up the clergy are ignorant of scripture because they do not even bother to read the Holy Scriptures. They cannot teach members of their congregations the truth of the Gospel because they are truly ignorant of it themselves. Many pastors, priests, and bishops have not read through the Holy Scriptures, have no knowledge of the covenants, and simply broadcast their opinions each week from the pulpit of their churches. Jesus commented on this blindness in the book of Matthew by saying, *"... And if the blind lead the blind, both shall fall into the ditch."(KJV, Matthew 15:14)*

The Levitical Priesthood and the Law of Moses served an important role in bringing us to the salvation we now enjoy through the death and resurrection of Jesus. If there had not been an old covenant in Israel, there would be no new covenant with the entire world. If there had been no works of the law for the atonement of sin, we would not have this dispensation of grace, and if the Levitical priesthood did not exist we would not have Jesus as our High Priest. The New Testament emerged from the Old.

6

The Personal Relationship With Jesus

To the born again believer, the New Testament or new covenant established by the death, burial, and resurrection of Jesus, did not just establish a new religion called Christianity, it also gave birth to the personal spiritual relationship with Jehovah and His son Jesus. This spiritual intimacy, more than any other factor, is what defines the new covenant. Under the Old Testament, Israel worshipped Jehovah through the offering of sacrifices, the observing of feast days, and through the many ordinances contained in the Law of Moses. They went up to Jerusalem each year to have offerings made for their sins and to atone for their many transgressions of the laws of Jehovah; they could not approach Jehovah directly with their offering, neither could they have their sins blotted out without going through the priests.

Though they worshipped Jehovah, they did not experience the intimacy that Jehovah requires us to share with Him and it is fair to say that because this intimacy was lacking, many in Israel strayed from Jehovah's righteousness.

The death of Jesus and the fulfillment of the laws of Moses brought this estrangement to its end. Jesus opened the door to intimacy with Jehovah to all humanity. Jehovah would no more seem far away; the guilt of sin would no more have to be carried until a priest offered a sin offering once per year at the temple in Jerusalem, and no one would be dependent on earthly priests for access to Jehovah.

Humans were at last free to approach Jehovah directly through Jesus and sins could be forgiven immediately as long as forgiveness was requested. Free at last! Free at last! Thank God Almighty we are free at last! We were free to establish and build a personal relationship with Jesus and Jehovah, free from the restrictions of the Law of Moses, free from the crushing weight that sin has on the conscience, free from the fear of death and hell! Yes! We were finally free through the shed blood of our Lord and Savior Jesus Christ, the only son of the living God Jehovah.

To ensure that this freedom was understood, Jesus extended several invitations to humans to come and share an intimate relationship with Him. The first invitation is recorded in the book of Matthew, *"Come to me, all you who are troubled and weighted down with care, and I will give you rest. Take my yoke on you and become like me, for I am gentle and without pride, and you will have rest for your souls; For my yoke is good, and the weight I take up is not hard."(BBE, Matthew 11:28-30)*

Here we see Jesus extending an invitation to those of us that are troubled and weighted down with the cares of this life. It cannot be denied that this life is a cruel existence and at best can only be described as an experience in pain, tragedy, and tears with brief moments of happiness interspersed in an otherwise sad existence. We are stalked by fear, burdened by guilt, and hounded by trouble. Even the few that are financially able to care well for themselves and are not in need of any material resource, struggle with the spiritual void within and the endless questions about the purpose of life.

To so many, life seems pointless and an absolute waste of time and the hopelessness that descends upon them often leads them to suicide or deep depression. There is truly no lasting happiness or peace to be found in this world. Even in love we find pain and in our joys we often experience sorrows.

In response to all these things, Jesus invites us to give all our sorrows, pain, sadness, guilt, troubles, financial hardships, fears, and hopelessness to Him and in exchange He will give us rest. Jesus replaces all our pain and sorrows with His perfect peace. Peace is the only antidote for inner turmoil and troubles of the mind. It is also the only antidote to a guilty conscience and a fearful existence.

I once heard a television celebrity declare his fear of death on national television. Here is a man with great financial resources and influence, name recognition and worldwide acclaim and yet he lives a fearful existence, dreading the day he will be no more and uncertain about his eternal destiny. Jesus died for this man also and is extending His offer of peace to him and all who are like him.

The personal relationship with Jesus grants us the privilege of giving to Jesus all our concerns and then not being concerned about them. I often describe it as worry free living; living peacefully even though all hell is breaking out around us. Jesus describes this as *"rest for your souls."*

There are many names throughout the Holy Scriptures used to describe Jesus. He is called the *"Almighty God,"* the *"Everlasting Father,"* *"Counsellor,"* and *"Wonderful"*. Most notably, however, Jesus is called *"The Prince of Peace."* The prophet Isaiah, in foretelling of the coming and birth of Jesus attributes to Him all the aforementioned names in the book of Isaiah, *"For unto us a child is born, unto us a son is given: and the government shall be upon his shoulder: and his name shall be called Wonderful, Counsellor, The mighty God, The everlasting Father, The Prince of Peace."(KJV, Isaiah 9:6)*

Jesus is indeed the Prince of Peace and without Him there is no peace. Because Jesus is the embodiment of Jehovah, He is here described as a prince only because Jehovah is the King of all the earth and universe. Access to Jehovah cannot be obtained except through Jesus. As we have seen before, the death of Jesus ended the Levitical priesthood and ended access to Jehovah through the priests of the tribe of Levi. Jesus then became the High Priest for all humanity, and the only access to Jehovah. Jesus made this clear when He stated, *"I am the way, the truth, and the life!"* ... *"Without me, no one can go to the Father."(CEV, John 14:6)* The peace that comes from Jehovah can therefore be only accessed through Jesus. Jesus then becomes humanity's only source for peace as peace is not natural to the earth. Peace is not natural to the earth because all humans were born in sin with the devil as our spiritual father. The devil is described as a murderer and a liar, not the source of peace. It is little wonder that the earth is in such turmoil. There are famines, wars, pestilences, diseases, death, and destruction everywhere. Humanity reflects the personality of their father the devil and the manifestation of that personality is evident in the deeds of mankind.

Jesus, on the other hand, brings peace to the believer and to all who accept Him as their Lord and Savior. The world's religions, philosophies, and political systems cannot give peace as the world does not know peace. No one can give what they do not possess. Before ascending to heaven, Jesus said to the Apostles, *"I give you peace, the kind of peace that only I can give. It isn't like the peace that this world can give. So don't be worried or afraid."(CEV, John 14:27)*

The peace that Jesus offers to us cannot be found in this world but only in Him. It cannot be purchased with money, material possessions cannot give it, and neither can it be found in sexual relationships of any kind. The peace of Jesus is a heavenly peace sent by Jehovah through His son. It defies this world and triumphs over all earthly trials and troubles. It is a peace that cannot be comprehended by the natural man as it is spiritual and from a spiritual source.

The Holy Scriptures describe it as a peace that cannot be fully understood by man and that is deeper than all knowledge. It keeps the believers hearts and minds guarded against the troubles of this world and grants the believer a divine assurance that all is well. It is described in the New Testament book of Philippians 4:7, *"And the peace of God, which passeth all understanding, shall keep your hearts and minds through Christ Jesus."(KJV, Philippians 4:7)*

Each born again believer has access to this peace through a personal relationship with Jesus, a personal relationship that begins by accepting Jesus as Lord and personal Savior. Salvation is a gift from Jehovah that is extended to all mankind. It was purchased by the shed blood of Jesus and is available to all who will receive it. It is of no benefit to those who do not believe it as it can only be received through faith (faith is looked at in great detail later in this chapter). The steps to accepting Jesus as one's personal Lord and Savior are outlined below as are the steps to being born again.

1. The personal relationship with Jesus begins with calling upon the name of the Lord. The following scriptures state this clearly:

   a. Romans 10:13 *"For whosoever shall call upon the name of the Lord shall be saved."(KJV)*

   b. Acts 2:21 *"And it shall come to pass, that whosoever shall call on the name of the Lord shall be saved."(KJV)*

   c. John 10:9 *"I am the door: by me if any man enter in, he shall be saved..."(KJV)*

Calling upon the name of the Lord is an acknowledgement that Jesus is the only begotten son of Jehovah and that salvation can only come through Him and no other. It is also an acknowledgement that access to Jehovah is only through Jesus and no other. Besides being an acknowledgement of Jesus' authority and power to grant salvation, it is also the believer's acknowledgement of their sins and the need to have them forgiven by Jesus.

It is a prerequisite to the personal relationship with Jesus that the sinner goes to Jesus prayer and call upon His name to receive salvation.

2. The second step to the personal relationship with Jesus is being baptized. Acknowledgement that Jesus is the son of Jehovah and that He died for the sins of

mankind, and that calling upon Him for forgiveness of sins will result in forgiveness of the believers' sins, must be followed with baptism. One cannot call upon the name of the Lord and then stop at that point. The Holy Scriptures make clear that baptism is a necessary step. The following excerpted verses illustrate this point:

a. Mark 16:16 *"He that believeth and is baptized shall be saved; but he that believeth not shall be damned."(KJV)*

b. Acts 22:16 *". . . arise, and be baptized, and wash away thy sins, calling on the name of the Lord."(KJV)*

c. Acts 2:38 *"Then Peter said unto them, Repent, and be baptized every one of you in the name of Jesus Christ for the remission of sins. . ."(KJV)*

Baptism in water involves being fully immersed in water in the name of the Lord Jesus for the remission or washing away of sins. Having water poured over ones head, as stated before, is not baptism and will not satisfy the requirement for being baptized. The personal relationship with Jesus requires complete immersion in water during baptism.

3. The third step to the personal relationship with Jesus is conversion. Conversion requires the new believer to change the way they live. The former sinful lifestyle has to be abandoned and rejected. A homosexual could no longer engage in homosexual relationships and neither could an adulterer continue an adulterous affair. The unmarried believer could not engage in a sexual relationship unless they got married and an abuser

of drugs could no longer continue in that lifestyle of addiction. All sinful practices would have to be brought to its end. Conversion occurs through a complete renewal of mind and spirit. The following scriptures outline this.

a. Romans 12:2 *"And be not conformed to this world: but be ye transformed by the renewing of your mind, that ye may prove what is that good, and acceptable, and perfect, will of God."(KJV)*

b. 2 Corinthians 5:17 *"Anyone who belongs to Christ is a new person. The past is forgotten, and everything is new."(CEV)*

c. Ephesians 4:22-23 *" . . . put away, in relation to your earlier way of life, the old man, which has become evil by love of deceit; And be made new in the spirit of your mind"(BBE)*

Conversion requires change, a complete change in thought and conduct. Jesus will not have a personal relationship with anyone still living a lifestyle of sin. He requires repentance and transformation.

It must be acknowledged that mere human effort cannot accomplish the transformation and conversion that is required for us to enter a personal relationship with Jesus. We were born in sin with the devil as our spiritual father. It is extremely difficult if not sometimes impossible to ignore the sinful desires of the flesh. The flesh has dominion over us, a dominion that can only be broken by the power of Jehovah. This is the legacy of sin. Jehovah created us to have dominion over all things including ourselves, as was discussed previously in our look at creation. We were given dominion over the earth and all that is in it.

When Adam and Eve sinned against Jehovah, this order was reversed. We lost dominion over the earth and over ourselves. We entered into a struggle with the earth, the animals, and the elements. The most formidable struggle we entered into, however, was the struggle with ourselves. The flesh would no longer be subjected to us; instead it would war against us.

It is important to remember that we are not our bodies, we simply inhabit our bodies. We are spirits living in bodies. This struggle with the flesh is carefully documented in the Holy Scriptures and without the power of Jehovah that comes through Jesus, we will not be successful in our struggle against our bodies.

The book of 1Peter 2:11 warns the believers to *"... keep yourselves from the desires of the flesh which make war against the soul,"* (BBE) and in the book of Romans 7:14-20, the Apostle Paul documents his own struggle with his flesh:

"For we are conscious that the law is of the spirit; but I am of the flesh, given into the power of sin. And I have no clear knowledge of what I am doing, for that which I have a mind to do, I do not, but what I have hate for, that I do. But, if I do that which I have no mind to do, I am in agreement with the law that the law is good. So it is no longer I who do it, but the sin living in me. For I am conscious that in me, that is, in my flesh, there is nothing good: I have the mind but not the power to do what is right. For the good which I have a mind to do, I do not: but the evil which I have no mind to do, that I do. But if I do what I have no mind to do, it is no longer I who do it, but the sin living in me."(BBE)

Here the Apostle Paul documents and outlines his own struggle with his flesh; a struggle all born again believers go through and indeed all mankind. The human body is sinful and delights in sinful things. It is in a constant state of rebellion against Jehovah and His spiritual laws. The human spirit engages in a constant struggle to reestablish dominion and authority over the body, knowing that the sinful nature of the flesh leads to death and destruction. This spiritual dominion over the body was lost through sin.

The Apostle Paul laments this sad state that all humans are in, this struggle against sin. He continues through to verse 24 of the book of Romans, identifying sin in his body as the cause of his struggle. He acknowledges a *"law of sin"* which dwells in his flesh and rhetorically asks the question, *"Who will free me from this body of death?"*

"So I see a law that, though I have a mind to do good, evil is present in me. In my heart I take pleasure in the law of God, But I see another law in my body, working against the law of my mind, and making me the servant of the law of sin which is in my flesh. How unhappy am I! who will make me free from the body of this death?"(BBE)

As seen in Paul's lamentations about himself we cannot free ourselves from the curse of sin that lives in our bodies, only Jesus can deliver us from this curse. It is for this reason that we call upon the name of Jesus as the first step in establishing our personal relationship with Him. The Holy Scriptures state that He gives us power to become the children of Jehovah, power to overcome ourselves, *"But as many as received him, to them gave he power to become the sons of God, even to them that believe on his name: Which were born, not of blood, nor of the will of the flesh, nor of the will of man, but of God."(KJV, John 1:12-13)*

The personal relationship with Jesus is an essential element of salvation. Indeed, it is true to state that no one can be saved without it. Jesus requires that we love Him as without loving Him we cannot serve Him nor do His will. This is a distinct characteristic of Christianity and the Christian relationship; it is characterized by love. The born again believer does not *"join"* the religion, he or she becomes *"born of God."* The Christian religion is not appended to the believers' life, it becomes their life. The born again believer is in a relationship with Jesus twenty four hours a day. There is never a time that the believer is outside of this relationship as the Christian religion is a depiction of the love story between Jehovah and mankind.

Jesus summarized it in these words, *"Thou shalt love the Lord thy God with all thy heart, and with all thy soul, and with all thy mind."(KJV, Matthew 22:37)* Jesus must be our preoccupation, we must be focused on loving Him at all times. We are commanded to love Him as without loving Him we cannot keep Jehovah's commandments. Jesus makes this clear in the book of John 14:15, *"If ye love me, keep my commandments."(KJV)* It is absolutely impossible to keep the commandments of Jehovah without having a personal, intimate, love relationship with Him and His son Jesus. Jesus died for the sins of humanity and opened the doors of salvation because of love. It was Jehovah's love for us that led to the death of Jesus. The Holy Scriptures informs us that Jesus did not die for Himself as He was without sin. Instead it was Jehovah's love for mankind that led Jehovah to offer up Jesus as a sacrificial lamb for the sins of the world. Christianity was founded in love, Jehovah's love for humanity, *"For God so loved the world, that he gave his only begotten Son, that whosoever believeth in him should not perish, but have everlasting life."(KJV, John 3:16)*

Jehovah demonstrated His love for us through the personal sacrifice of His son Jesus and in appreciation for this sacrifice, and as a response to His love we are commanded to love Him. This is not optional. To be saved we must enter into a personal love relationship with the Lord.

Can Homosexuals Have a Personal Relationship with Jesus?

Homosexuality is not new. It's been a part of societies since the fall of man. Just as adultery, fornication (sex outside of marriage), lying, stealing, covetousness, and violating the weekly Sabbath day are all sins before Jehovah, so is homosexuality a sin before Jehovah. Sin is not new to the earth and the existence of humanity and neither is homosexuality. What is new, however, is the stance of many churches that approve of homosexuality as a gift and state that is was given to some by Jehovah. Churches have ordained practicing homosexuals as bishops and priests and there are openly homosexual couples that are being told by churches that Jehovah does not condemn their lifestyle and that they will be saved as they are. They inform them that there is nothing to repent of with regards to the homosexual lifestyle and many clergy seek to reinterpret the Holy Scriptures to conform to this new dogma.

The true believers in Jesus who seek to point out the errors of the homosexual lifestyle are often attacked and accused of being homophobic and of being intolerant. They are accused of being hateful, divisive, and of spreading hate.

Homosexuality has become a "hot button" issue in churches and the society at large. Many even dare compare the homosexual agenda today with the civil rights agenda of the 1950s and 1960s. With all this "sound and fury" about homosexuality and the rights of homosexuals in churches and the society, many Christians have been intimidated into accepting this sinful practice as acceptable and as righteous. Not wanting to be seen as discriminatory, many have embraced this sin and have blessed it as righteous. There are even those who claim that Jehovah created homosexuals to be that way. *"How can Jehovah condemn someone when He created them like this?"* is their rationale for justifying the homosexual lifestyle.

In this chapter, I will reiterate the stance the Holy Scriptures has outlined regarding this and will also highlight why a practicing homosexual cannot have a personal relationship with Jesus and why practicing homosexuals must be converted to be saved.

The Holy Scriptures, as we have already seen, identifies homosexuality as a sinful practice. We have also seen that under the Law of Moses the penalty for engaging in homosexual conduct was death by stoning. Under the New Testament or new covenant established by the shed blood of Jesus, the Apostle Paul once again identifies homosexuality as an abominable sin against Jehovah, and throughout the New Testament books we've seen the practice condemned many times by various Apostles and disciples.

There is nowhere in the Holy Scriptures that approval can be found for this sinful lifestyle. Since the only authoritative source a Christian has for guidance is the Holy Scriptures, a Christian is not being homophobic in stating that homosexuality is sinful. He or she is being truthful. Christians are not being fearful of homosexuals and are not being discriminatory in stating what the Holy Scriptures have already stated clearly. To state homosexuality is sinful and unacceptable to Jehovah is in fact an act of righteousness.

The Holy Scriptures are the only authoritative source for Christian doctrines and beliefs because without the Holy Scriptures (both Old and New Testaments), there would be no Christian religion. The tenets of Christianity are based solely on the Bible and on no other book. Whatever the Holy Scriptures condemns as sinful, becomes sinful to the Christian, and whatever the Holy Scriptures approves as righteous, becomes righteous to the Christian. There is no room for opinion or personal input with regards to Christian doctrine.

This is necessarily true because humans are evil in nature and righteousness is not natural to us. During the days of Noah, Jehovah summed up humanity in the following verse of the book of Genesis, *"...the wickedness of man was great in the earth, and ... every imagination of the thoughts of his heart was only evil continually."(KJV, Genesis 6:5)*

Humans were evil then, and humans are evil now. Jesus declared that just as humanity was evil in the days of Noah, they would be just as evil towards the time of His second coming, *"When the Son of Man appears, things will be just as they were when Noah lived."(CEV, Matthew 24:37)*

The Holy Scriptures further informs us that righteousness is of Jehovah, that is, He is the author of what righteousness is. This is found in the book of Daniel, *"O Lord, righteousness belongeth unto thee..."* *(KJV, Daniel 9:27)* Since Jehovah is the author of righteousness, we cannot declare anything righteous as we have no authority to do so. Public opinion does not have an impact on what Jehovah declares righteous. If a sinful lifestyle has suddenly become popular and acceptable to the society, it does not impact Jehovah's judgment on it as sin.

In the book of Malachi, Jehovah declares, *"...I am the LORD All-Powerful, and I never change..." (CEV, Malachi 3:6)*; this makes clear to us that Jehovah will not change His stance on an issue of morality. What He declares to be immoral will remain immoral forever and what He declares to be righteous will be righteous forever.

Jehovah's righteousness is not changed because of pressure from public opinion.

Homosexuality was not declared sinful by humans, it was declared sinful by Jehovah. The fact that public opinion has shifted and now regard homosexuals as being *"gifted"* and as being *"born"* that way does not impact Jehovah's position in any way. Biblical scholars and members of the clergy that are embracing homosexuals as saints are in the process of creating their own religion as they have stepped outside the boundaries outlined by Jehovah. They are seeking to establish their own righteousness and to create their own laws.

Righteousness does not belong to us and we cannot create it. We are simply told what it is and are obliged to obey it. With that said, it must also be stated that Jehovah loves the homosexual as He loves all the sinners of the world. The Holy Scriptures state, *"For God so loved the world, that he gave his only begotten Son, that whosoever believeth in him should not perish, but have everlasting life."(KJV, John 3:16)* This is the basic message to all the people of the world. God loves us all! He loves the homosexual just as He loves anyone else. In the same way He extends His love to all, including the homosexual, He extends the opportunity to repent of our sinful lifestyles to all, including the homosexual.

Adultery, fornication, and bestiality (sexual relations between humans and animals) are all sexual sins that no one dares to justify as righteous acts. Homosexuality is also a sexual sin and no one should dare justify it as a righteous act. What member of the clergy would suggest that sleeping with another man's wife is a gift that Jehovah has given to some or that having sex with animals is a gift that Jehovah has given to some? Since these sins cannot be justified, why then is there such an effort to justify homosexuality as a righteous

act? At best homosexuality is fornication as most homosexuals are
not married and are engaged in sexual relationships outside of the
sanctity of the matrimonial bond. At worst it is an abominable act as
two people of the same sex are not permitted by Jehovah to engage
in a sexual relationship. There is nothing righteous or virtuous about
homosexuality and it is certainly not a gift from Jehovah.

Homosexuals should be wary of clergy members who misinform
them that they can enter the kingdom of Jehovah as they are or escape
the pain of hell as they are. Jesus warns us that hell is a literal place of
fire and eternal torment created for the devil and his fallen angels. It
is not a place that was created for mankind. Sinful men and women
who do not accept Jesus as their personal Savior and who do not turn
away from their sinful lifestyle, will spend all eternity there. Eternity
has no time, it is forever. Jesus warns that there will be *weeping and
gnashing of teeth,*" an expression that tells us there will be great wailing
and sorrow.

There are many in our society today who will no doubt read
this book and label it homophobic and intolerant. This is not
unusual, especially among clergy members seeking to gain the favor
of the homosexual community. This has happened before. For
the homosexual who may read this book, they should know that
informing them of the truth is not intolerance or homophobia
but love.

Jesus states that only the truth can make one free and a homosexual
cannot be free from the bondage of homosexuality unless this truth
is received by him or her. *"Coming out"* of the closet and seeking
acceptance as is, accomplishes nothing. Believing a lie that Jehovah
has blessed homosexuals with a special gift will not remove the
guilt of sin. The truth, as stated throughout the Holy Scriptures,

is that homosexuality is sinful to Jehovah and must be confessed as sin by the homosexual. Like every other sinful lifestyle, it must be repented of, the homosexual must be baptized, and a rejecting of the lifestyle must occur, before a personal relationship can be established with Jesus.

There is the well known story, told in the Holy Scriptures, of the woman that was caught in the act of adultery. The Law of Moses was clear regarding the penalty for such an act; she was to be stoned to death. Jesus, however, in showing her mercy and extending the grace of Jehovah to her, informed her accusers that they could carry out the penalty if they were guiltless of any sin. Since all mankind are sinners, they all walked away leaving the woman alone with Jesus. Jesus then said to the woman, "... go, and sin no more."(KJV, John 8:11) It is important to note from this story, that Jesus identified her adultery as sin; He did not approve of her act but instead gave her the opportunity to turn from that lifestyle. The same is to be said for homosexuality; Jehovah does identify it as sin and does not approve of it. He instead has given homosexuals the opportunity to turn away from this lifestyle.

Homosexuals who have turned away from the homosexual lifestyle and have identified it as sinful can have a personal relationship with Jesus. In their converted and renewed state they are no longer homosexuals. Practicing homosexuals, however, cannot have a personal relationship with Jesus.

What Is Faith?

What is faith and why is it important to the personal relationship with Jesus? The definition provided us by the Holy Scriptures is found in the book of Hebrews, *"Faith makes us sure of what we hope for and gives us proof of what we cannot see."(CEV, Hebrews 11:1)* This definition tells us that faith gives us certainty about our hope and provides us with evidence of that which is invisible.

Since Christianity is based on the worship of Jehovah, a Spirit that cannot be seen, and Jesus His son, a historical figure that we have never interacted with, our only proof of their existence is our faith. Our faith gives us the assurance that the invisible Jehovah is real and that the historical figure called Jesus is truly His son. It is because we cannot see God why we need to believe in God. To truly understand the importance of faith and to understand its definition we will take a look at the word hope, a word that we can all relate to.

In our natural existence we live by hope. We go to work each day being sure that we'll receive a paycheck at the end of the week or at the end of every two weeks. We dedicatedly wake up each morning, dress ourselves, and spend our own money for food, gas, bus fares, train fares, and all the other expenditures that go along with going out to work. We do this without question, believing in a paycheck that may or may not materialize.

There are those of us who even borrow from others and guarantee them repayment on a certain future date based simply on our hope of getting paid. We embrace our hope of getting paid at a specific time not as an uncertainty but as a guaranteed certainty. But why are we certain? There truly is no guarantee that we'll be paid. Companies go bankrupt all the time and business fail all the time. Many people have made retirement plans, purchased luxury items, taken out mortgages, and made personal investments in corporations that have failed. What was thought was a sure thing turned out not to be.

The recent case of corporate giant Enron's collapse and bankruptcy is enough to make this point. Though we approach things in our daily life as guarantees, we really have no reason to be so assured that they are. What we are doing in our daily lives is called living by hope; approaching the uncertain as though it was a certainty and approaching the invisible (the not yet received paycheck) as though it were already reality.

We approach receiving a paycheck as certain because of our hope. We buy things on credit and take out mortgages because of our hope. We have no proof we'll be able to pay for these expenditures but our hope gives us the assurance that we'll be able to. Without hope we will not be able to live. Hope allows us to embrace invisible things and to accept them as real. Accepting the future (invisible) paycheck as real then allows us to make purchases as though the money already existed when in fact we are making our purchases only on our hope. Our hope allows us to live in the future. This is the same for faith.

Faith allows us to accept a reality that we have no material evidence of, but nevertheless live with, as though the material reality was already present. This is why the Holy Scriptures say that faith makes us sure of our hope. In the example of the paycheck, we hoped for a paycheck but lived our lives as if we already had that paycheck. We made the paycheck real by our hope and it became real because of our hope. Faith does the same, it makes us certain of what we hope for and that certainty creates the material reality or evidence of what we hoped for.

Let us look again at the definition of faith and make a few creative substitutions in the definition using our paycheck example.

Original Scriptural definition:

"Faith makes us sure of what we hope for and gives us proof of what we cannot see."(Hebrews 11:1)

Our definition with substitution:

"Faith makes us sure of a paycheck we hope for and gives us proof of a paycheck we cannot see."

From this example, we see that faith is then our hope in action. A hope that allows us to treat the invisible as real and also allows us the power to create the invisible reality into material substance. This is the reason faith is important to Jehovah. Without faith we can accomplish nothing.

Let us take a brief look at what occurs in the absence of faith using the same example of the paycheck. Without believing we'll be paid no one would go to work. No one would get up early each morning, dress themselves, incur traveling expenses, or borrow from others if they had no hope of a paycheck. There would be no purchases, no mortgages, and no investments. People would be living in fear and they would do nothing. The absence of hope would create paralysis. The absence of hope prevents the investment of effort and thereby becomes a self fulfilling prophecy of the individual's future. The entire society would come to a screeching halt if there were suddenly no hope. Humanity lives by hope and all economies operate on hope. It is the essential fuel that allows us to be creative, to be happy, to raise families, to build business, and to do all that human societies do. If hope is gone then all is gone.

Faith is our hope in action. A hope that guarantees us a bright future and allows us to get up and go, assuring us that hope will allow the invisible to become real. This is also true of our relationship with Jehovah and His son Jesus Christ. We must first believe in Jehovah and Jesus to know Jehovah and Jesus. Facts follow faith. We believe first and then receive evidence of our faith afterwards.

In the same way we have faith for a paycheck and a paycheck becomes a reality (a material fact), it is the same way we exercise our faith in Jehovah and Jesus and we will know Jehovah and Jesus. Without faith we cannot have a relationship with Jesus and without faith we cannot be saved. The Holy Scriptures informs us that if we have no faith we cannot be pleasing to Jehovah, *"But without faith no one can please God. We must believe that God is real..." (CEV, Hebrews 11:6)* This is true as we must first believe He is real before we can relate to Him as real. The personal relationship with Jesus is built on faith and can only grow on faith.

Faith can be described as the key that releases the power of Jehovah into the lives of the believers. Indeed, Jesus makes the point that faith makes the impossible possible and overcomes all obstacles.

Jesus taught the Apostles much about faith and often berated them on their lack of faith. In teaching the Apostles that they should not concern themselves with their daily needs, that is, they should not worry about such things, Jesus informed them that their faith in Jehovah would ensure that their daily needs are taken care of. This is recorded in the book of Matthew:

*"God gives such beauty to everything that grows in the fields, even though it
is here today and thrown into a fire tomorrow. He will surely do even more for
you! Why do you have such little faith? Don't worry and ask yourselves, "Will we
have anything to eat? Will we have anything to drink? Will we have any clothes to
wear?" Only people who don't know God are always worrying about such things.
Your Father in heaven knows that you need all of these. But more than anything
else, put God's work first and do what he wants. Then the other things will be yours
as well. Don't worry about tomorrow. It will take care of itself."(CEV, Matthew
6:30-34)*

Here Jesus informs us that we should live by our faith as Jehovah
is our provider and will take care of us. It is His power that ensures
that we live, that we eat, that we are clothed, that we are housed, and
that we are taken care of generally. This reduces our responsibility
in our personal relationship with Jesus to that of simply putting
our hope in Him in action. Remember that faith is hope in action.
We are therefore simply called upon to have faith in Him for our
daily needs.

The reason we are cautioned against worrying is because worrying
is a manifestation of fear. People who are certain of the future will
never worry about the future. Certainty eliminates fear and thereby
eliminates worry. Worry is another way of stating that we have no
faith. The believer in Jesus that is engaged in a personal relationship
with Him has nothing to be concerned about. He or she is guaranteed
a secure and bright future and is only required to believe it. As was
pointed out before, fact follows faith. What is believed will inevitably
manifest as material fact.

Jesus made clear to the Apostles that when they made a request in
prayer to Jehovah, they must first believe that whatever they requested
is already given to them, even before receiving it. If they believe they

are already in possession of it then it will be given to them. This is what Jesus said, *"Therefore I say unto you, What things soever ye desire, when ye pray, believe that ye receive them, and ye shall have them."(KJV, Mark 11:24).*

Here again we see the demonstration of fact following faith. To demonstrate more clearly, let us look at the example of a believer asking Jehovah to provide them a job. After making this request in prayer, the believer is then required to start believing that they have gotten the job, even though their present reality is that of being unemployed. Whenever they pray they should not be asking again for a job, but instead should be offering prayers of thanksgiving for the job they believe they already have received.

Giving thanks for the job demonstrates the believer's confidence in the hope that Jehovah has answered their prayer and has already provided the job requested. It is this faith that will result in the receiving of the job. Faith that prayer has been answered without having material evidence that it has been answered will result in the manifested evidence of whatever was requested.

Jesus reiterates this as He spoke to the Apostles in the following text excerpted from the book of Matthew 17, *"... If you had faith no larger than a mustard seed, you could tell this mountain to move from here to there. And it would. Everything would be possible for you."(CEV, Matthew 17:20)*

Faith makes all things possible and there is nothing that can withstand its power. It is the foundation upon which all things are built and it is the only reason for living. Jehovah demonstrated the power of faith as He created the world. He did not create the world with His hands; He instead created the world with His words. In the book of Genesis the events of creation are outlined. The following is an excerpt of these events:

"In the beginning God created the heavens and the earth. The earth was barren, with no form of life; it was under a roaring ocean covered with darkness. But the Spirit of God was moving over the water. God said, "I command light to shine!" And light started shining. God looked at the light and saw that it was good. He separated light from darkness and named the light "Day" and the darkness "Night." Evening came and then morning--that was the first day. God said, "I command a dome to separate the water above it from the water below it." And that's what happened. God made the dome and named it "Sky." Evening came and then morning--that was the second day. God said, "I command the water under the sky to come together in one place, so there will be dry ground." And that's what happened. God named the dry ground Land," and he named the water "Ocean." God looked at what he had done and saw that it was good. God said, "I command the earth to produce all kinds of plants, including fruit trees and grain." And that's what happened. The earth produced all kinds of vegetation. God looked at what he had done, and it was good. Evening came and then morning--that was the third day. God said, "I command lights to appear in the sky and to separate day from night and to show the time for seasons, special days, and years. I command them to shine on the earth." And that's what happened." (CEV, Genesis 1:1-15)

Note from the excerpted text that Jehovah simply commanded things to be and they were. This is a true demonstration of the power of faith. Jehovah commanded something to be in existence that never existed, He believed that it was in existence because He had commanded it, and it materialized into existence in obedience to Jehovah's faith. This is what Jesus meant when He said nothing is impossible to those who have faith. We can command the mountains in our lives to move and they will move in obedience to our faith. It is faith that commands the universe and we have been authorized to harness faith's great potential.

The absence of faith creates hopelessness, and hopelessness creates despair and depression. Despair and depression creates mental, physical, and spiritual paralysis. It is for this reason that faith is the essential ingredient in the personal relationship with Jesus. Our faith activates our hopes and generates the necessary enthusiasm for living. Faith propels our ideas forward and provides us with inspiration. It allows us to take steps we would not otherwise have taken and to face challenges that otherwise would have left us cringing. It is no wonder Jehovah is upset with those who cannot or refuse to believe. They deny the very power of life itself! The Holy Scriptures state that those who cannot have faith or are not steadfast in their faith can receive nothing from Jehovah and it goes so far as to state that the unbelieving are unstable in all their ways. Here is the excerpted text from the book of James, *"But when you ask for something, you must have faith and not doubt. Anyone who doubts is like an ocean wave tossed around in a storm. If you are that kind of person, you can't make up your mind, and you surely can't be trusted. So don't expect the Lord to give you anything at all."(CEV, James 1:6-7)*

Faith in Jesus is the same as stating that you trust Jesus. Faith is hope in action and faith is also manifested trust. Trust is the foundation upon which all positive relationships are built. Without faith a relationship with Jesus is impossible and worshipping Jehovah is also impossible. As seen from the Biblical definition of faith, faith allows the believer in Jesus to embrace the invisible reality of Jehovah, to relate to the invisible reality of Jehovah, and to live in confidence in the invisible reality of Jehovah. Faith brings the invisible reality to appear as manifested material reality and allows us to live in a future that does not yet exist but already is real. Faith makes all things possible.

The Baptism with the Holy Spirit

Another very important component of the personal relationship with Jesus is the baptism with the Holy Spirit. The baptism with the Holy Spirit; what exactly it is, and how and when one is baptized with the Holy Spirit has caused much debate in the Christian community. Great care must be taken in any discussion about the Holy Spirit as Jesus warns that all sins will be forgiven a person except the sin of blasphemy against the Holy Spirit. This is a warning that must be taken very, very seriously. To blaspheme is *"to speak of or address with irreverence"* (Merriam -Webster dictionary), and therefore this warning has to be made clear during all discussions regarding the Holy Spirit as to be irreverent or disrespectful carries eternal consequences.

Jesus gave this warning while here on earth. He was being accused of having a demonic spirit by several Jewish teachers and issued this warning, *"I promise you that any of the sinful things you say or do can be forgiven, no matter how terrible those things are. But if you speak against the Holy Spirit, you can never be forgiven. That sin will be held against you forever."(CEV, Mark 3:28-29)* This text cautions us to proceed with our discussions on the Holy Spirit very carefully.

The Holy Spirit is the spirit of Jehovah and is referred to as *"He"* and not *"It"* as the Holy Spirit is not a thing. The Holy Spirit is mentioned throughout both the Old and New Testament books of the Bible and it is known that He was given to the prophets of Israel, several kings of Israel including King Saul and King David, and to various other individuals who were not prophets or kings.

The Holy Spirit is also associated with prophesying throughout the Old Testament as anyone upon whom He came would prophecy. The Holy Spirit empowers the person to whom He is given and is the believers' chief ally in the spiritual battle for the eternal destiny of man. Human beings have no power of themselves to overcome the desires of the flesh or of the body. Neither do we have the power to confront and overcome the spiritual power of Satan and his demonic spirits that roam the earth. The battle for the souls of human beings is not a natural battle but a spiritual battle, hence the need for the Holy Spirit in this war to attain righteousness through Jesus.

The giving of the Holy Spirit to believers at large and not just to a selected few such as prophets and kings was first prophesied in the Old Testament book of Joel. The Apostle Peter referenced this prophecy in his first sermon after the ascension of Jesus, on the day of Pentecost, in the New Testament book of Acts. In the book of Joel, Jehovah foretells through the prophet Joel of the giving of His Holy Spirit to all believers, *"... I will give my Spirit to everyone. Your sons and daughters will prophesy. Your old men will have dreams, and your young men will see visions. In those days I will even give my Spirit to my servants, both men and women."* (*CEV, Joel 2:28*)

This prophecy was fulfilled on the day of Pentecost (50th day after the Passover) when the Holy Spirit came down upon the Apostles in Jerusalem, causing them to speak to the people in languages they had not previously known, and which resulted in the beginning of the Christian church, as over three thousand men and women received Jesus as Lord and Savior and were baptized on that day.

The Holy Spirit *"coming upon"* the Apostles in this way is also known as being *"baptized with the Holy Spirit."* It was John the Baptist who first used the word "baptize" in reference to the giving of the

Holy Spirit to the believers in Jesus. This is recorded in the book of Matthew. John was baptizing believers who were repentant of their sins and during one such baptism, he spoke to his followers about the coming of Jesus saying, *"I baptize you with water so that you will give up your sins. But someone more powerful is going to come, and I am not good enough even to carry his sandals. He will baptize you with the Holy Spirit and with fire."(CEV, Matthew 3:11)*

Jesus, before His ascension to heaven, informed the Apostles of the coming of the Holy Spirit after His departure from the earth. The Holy Spirit, known throughout the scriptures as the *Comforter*, the *Holy Ghost*, and the *Spirit of Truth*, was to be sent by Jesus to the Apostles and the believers, only after His ascension. Jesus informed the Apostles of this while still on earth. He informed them that it was to their advantage that He return to Jehovah in heaven, as without His return the Holy Spirit would not come to them. This is recorded in the book of John, *"But I tell you that I am going to do what is best for you. That is why I am going away. The Holy Spirit cannot come to help you until I leave. But after I am gone, I will send the Spirit to you." (CEV, John 16:7)*

The purpose of the Holy Spirit was to give the Apostles and the believers power to combat the spiritual forces of evil on the earth; power to cast out demons from people possessed with demons, power to miraculously heal sickness and diseases, power to resurrect the dead back to life, and power to know the truth from the deceptive lies of Satan. This power was to be essential in the establishing of the Church of Jesus and also in distinguishing the Christian church from all other forms of religion.

The Christian church could not be established without spiritual power as the demonic forces of Satan were lying in wait to destroy it. Jesus had already promised the Apostles that hell would not be successful in seeking the destruction of the church. To ensure that the church was empowered, Jesus instructed the Apostles to wait in Jerusalem and not go out to preach the Gospel until the Holy Spirit had come and given them the power needed to do so. This occurred in the book of Acts chapter 2, and resulted in the birth of the church. The record of the birth of the church and the baptizing of the believers with the Holy Spirit is of such importance that I have excerpted the first sixteen verses of the second chapter of the book of Acts for the readers benefit:

"On the day of Pentecost all the Lord's followers were together in one place. Suddenly there was a noise from heaven like the sound of a mighty wind! It filled the house where they were meeting. Then they saw what looked like fiery tongues moving in all directions, and a tongue came and settled on each person there. The Holy Spirit took control of everyone, and they began speaking whatever languages the Spirit let them speak. Many religious Jews from every country in the world were living in Jerusalem. And when they heard this noise, a crowd gathered. But they were surprised, because they were hearing everything in their own languages. They were excited and amazed, and said: Don't all these who are speaking come from Galilee? Then why do we hear them speaking our very own languages? Some of us are from Parthia, Media, and Elam. Others are from Mesopotamia, Judea, Cappadocia, Pontus, Asia, Phrygia, Pamphylia, Egypt, parts of Libya near Cyrene, Rome, Crete, and Arabia. Some of us were born Jews, and others of us have chosen to be Jews. Yet we all hear them using our own languages to tell the wonderful things God has done. Everyone was excited and confused. Some of them even kept asking each other, "What does all this mean?" Others made fun of the Lord's followers and said, "They are drunk." Peter stood with the eleven apostles and spoke in a loud and clear voice to the crowd: Friends and everyone else living in Jerusalem, listen carefully to what I have to say! You are wrong to think that these people are drunk. After all, it is only nine o'clock in the morning. But this is what God had the prophet Joel say, "When the last days come, I will give my Spirit to everyone. Your sons and daughters will prophesy. Your young men will see visions, and your old men will have dreams. In

those days I will give my Spirit to my servants, both men and women, and they will prophesy."(CEV, Acts 2:1-16)

This record of the coming of the Holy Spirit to the New Testament believers allows us to extract the following important points about the baptism of the believer with the Holy Spirit:

1. The baptism of the believer with the Holy Spirit is an actual event that can be traced to a time and place. It is not an event that is assumed to have taken place without the believer knowing when it occurred and where it occurred. With water baptism, the believer can identify the place and time of the baptismal event, so too with the baptism with the Holy Spirit. In this case we can clearly state that the believers and the Apostles were baptized with the Holy Spirit in Jerusalem (the place), and it was on the day of Pentecost at about 9:00 a.m. (the time).

2. The baptism with the Holy Spirit empowered the believers with the ability to speak languages they were not previously schooled in, that is, they spoke in languages unknown to them. The Holy Scriptures later refers to this as *"unknown tongue."* From this we know that the ability to speak a language unknown to the believer is normal with the baptism with the Holy Spirit as it is the Holy Spirit that speaks through the believer and not the believer himself or herself.

3. There were those who observed this phenomenon (the baptism and speaking in unknown tongues) and declared that the Apostles and the believers were intoxicated with

144

alcoholic beverages. This informs us that their behavior must have been unusual and may have appeared to be lacking the usual decorum and formality associated with religious events. From this we can conclude that the behavior of the believer baptized with the Holy Spirit may not conform to religious decorum and formality and observers should not be surprised.

4.   The Holy Spirit took control of the Apostles and believers at the time of baptism. From this we know that the believer who receives the baptism with the Holy Spirit is not in control at the time of receiving this spiritual baptism and that their actions and speech are not being directed by them but by the Holy Spirit and thus is not predictable.

5.   The baptism with the Holy Spirit gives the believer the ability to prophecy, to see visions, and to receive dreams from Jehovah. This enhances the believers' relationship with Jehovah and Jesus as increasing communication increases intimacy.

To be baptized with the Holy Spirit is to have Jehovah living in the body of the believer. With the end of the Levitical Priesthood, the temple in Jerusalem lost all relevance to salvation and was destroyed by the Romans in A.D. 70 as Jesus had prophesied in the book of Matthew 24, *"After Jesus left the temple, his disciples came over and said, "Look at all these buildings!" Jesus replied, "Do you see these buildings? They will certainly be torn down! Not one stone will be left in place.""(CEV, Matthew 24:2)*

Jehovah had no more interest in an earthly temple as the believers' body was now to be the temple of Jehovah. Jehovah would now live in the bodies of believers through the baptism with the Holy Spirit. This would bring the believer into a new level of intimacy with Jesus and establish a greater personal bond between men and God. The Apostle Paul explains this in the book of I Corinthians, *"...know ye not that your body is the temple of the Holy Ghost which is in you, which ye have of God, and ye are not your own?" (KJV, 1 Corinthians 6: 19)*

The born again believer that has been baptized with the Holy Spirit has become the church of Jehovah, a living, breathing temple, and place of continuous worship in honor of Jesus and Jehovah. This established the personal relationship at its highest level.

There are many born again believers who have not experienced baptism with the Holy Spirit and there are many churches that misinform their members regarding the same. There is the false teaching that believers are automatically baptized with the Holy Spirit, even though they cannot tell when this baptism occurred or where it occurred. There are churches that teach that baptism with the Holy Spirit occurs immediately at the time of water baptism. This is also a falsehood as we'll see in looking at several instances in the Holy Scriptures. In the early days of the newly established Christian church, there were also many believers who were not baptized with the Holy Spirit. There are several recorded events in the Holy Scriptures where the Apostles encountered believers who had not had this experience and prayed for them that they should have this baptism. There were sometimes even entire churches that had not received the baptism with the Holy Spirit. We will look at a few of these encounters from the book of Acts and will also respond to a question commonly asked, *"What do I do if I've not been baptized with the Holy Spirit?"*

Jesus makes it clear to us that we should ask Jehovah for the baptism with the Holy Spirit. This is recorded in the book of Luke, *"As bad as you are, you still know how to give good gifts to your children. But your heavenly Father is even more ready to give the Holy Spirit to anyone who asks."(CEV, Luke 11:13)*

This is a very important point for anyone who has not been baptized with the Holy Spirit and desires a greater personal relationship with Jehovah. Jesus tells us to *"Ask, and it shall be given..."* (KJV, Matthew 7:7); we therefore have the responsibility to ask our Lord in faith for the baptism with the Holy Spirit. If we do not ask for this baptism, we will not receive it. We should also have the desire for a greater personal relationship with Him. It should be earnestly desired and should be a relationship we genuinely would like to cultivate. Just like any other relationship in life, the more it is worked at the better it becomes. Close intimate relationships do not just happen by themselves; they are instead desired and sought after. A husband cannot continually ignore his wife and in the end is upset at the absence of intimacy in the marriage. The same is true for a wife.

Intimacy is cultivated through conversation and through paying attention to the person you are in relationship with. This is true for friendships, marriages, and spiritual relationships. If believers desire a greater intimate relationship with their Savior, then they need to seek after it. Jehovah states this in the book of Jeremiah, *"And ye shall seek me, and find me, when ye shall search for me with all your heart."(KJV, Jeremiah 29:13)* Jehovah expects us to search after Him. He wants us to truly love Him enough to be searching after Him and desiring Him. Believers desiring the baptism with the Holy Spirit need also to desire Jesus and to search after Jesus with all their hearts.

147

As stated before, there are several encounters recorded in the Holy Scriptures that tells us of believers that were not baptized with the Holy Spirit. In each case that is presented the baptism with the Holy Spirit was received. In our first case, the Apostle Paul encountered believers that were not baptized with the Holy Spirit because they had not heard of the Holy Spirit:

*"...Paul traveled across the hill country to Ephesus, where he met some of the Lord's followers. He asked them, "When you put your faith in Jesus, were you given the Holy Spirit?""No!" they answered. "We have never even heard of the Holy Spirit." "Then why were you baptized?" Paul asked. They answered, "Because of what John [the Baptist] taught." Paul replied, "John baptized people so that they would turn to God. But he also told them that someone else was coming, and that they should put their faith in him. Jesus is the one that John was talking about." After the people heard Paul say this, they were baptized in the name of the Lord Jesus. Then Paul placed his hands on them. **The Holy Spirit was given to them, and they spoke unknown languages and prophesied.** There were about twelve men in this group."(CEV, Acts 19:1-7)*

In our first case we see that ignorance of the existence of the Holy Spirit prevented baptism with the Holy Spirit. There are many churches that do not teach their members about the baptism with the Holy Spirit and the result is that the members are ignorant about this baptism. Other churches misinform their members that this baptism automatically happens without them knowing. Here we see that these believers knew when they received the baptism with the Spirit and where they received the baptism with the Spirit. They also spoke in unknown languages and prophesied.

Our second case involves a larger body of people. The city of Samaria had received the Gospel of Jesus and many people there had been baptized but no one had received the baptism with the

Holy Spirit. This again tells us that the baptism with the Holy Spirit is not an automatic occurrence at water baptism. The believer can be baptized in water but not experience the baptism with the Holy Spirit.

The Apostles Peter and John went to the city of Samaria and prayed for the new believers and they received the baptism with the Holy Spirit. Here is the scriptural account, *"Now when the Apostles at Jerusalem had news that the people of Samaria had taken the word of God into their hearts, they sent to them Peter and John; Who, when they came there, made prayer for them, that the Holy Spirit might be given to them: For up to that time he had not come on any of them; only baptism had been given to them in the name of the Lord Jesus. Then they put their hands on them, and the Holy Spirit came on them."(BBE, Acts 14-17)*

Here again we can identify the moment of receiving this baptism and also the time of the baptism. It is also seen that the Apostles Peter and John knew the baptism had occurred. We have seen in both cases that the believers received the Holy Spirit after being prayed for by the Apostles. In the first case we saw the Apostle Paul pray for the baptism with the Holy Spirit and in the second case we saw the Apostles Peter and John pray with the same results.

In our third and final case we'll see the first Gentile believers receive the baptism with the Holy Spirit prior to being baptized with water but immediately after the Gospel of Jesus was preached to them. This occurred in the house of Cornelius, a Roman Centurion, who without formally being taught about Jehovah, loved Jehovah and was a devout man. Jesus instructed Peter in a dream to go to his house and preach the Gospel to him and all the members of his household.

The following verses from the book of Acts tell the story of his entire household being baptized with the Holy Spirit, *"While Peter was still speaking, the Holy Spirit took control of everyone who was listening. Some Jewish followers of the Lord had come with Peter, and they were surprised that the Holy Spirit had been given to Gentiles. Now they were hearing Gentiles speaking unknown languages and praising God. Peter said, "These Gentiles have been given the Holy Spirit, just as we have! I am certain that no one would dare stop us from baptizing them." Peter ordered them to be baptized in the name of Jesus Christ, and they asked him to stay on for a few days."(CEV, Acts 10:44-48)*

Again the common elements of this spiritual event are:

1. The time the spiritual baptism occurred is known (during Peter's sermon).

2. The place the spiritual baptism occurred is known (Cornelius' house).

3. The witnesses to the baptism were able to tell the baptism occurred.

Believers who are misled into believing they have been baptized with the Holy Spirit and cannot identify these common elements should know with all certainty that they are NOT baptized with the Holy Spirit. This is not to say that believers that are not baptized with the Holy Spirit are not saved. Believing that Jesus is the Son of God, calling upon His name in repentance and being converted are the requirements for salvation. All believers that satisfy these requirements are certainly saved. The baptism with the Holy Spirit, however, enhances that experience and takes the believer to greater heights in their relationship with Jehovah.

The power of Jehovah comes through the Holy Spirit. The experience of speaking an unknown tongue or language, the power to cast out demonic spirits, the power to miraculously heal the sick, and the ability to raise the dead are all done through the power of the Holy Spirit. Those believers that are baptized with the Holy Spirit will experience more of the power of the Holy Spirit than those that are not. They will also experience more intimacy with Jehovah and ultimately will have greater faith than those that are not.

I'll complete this chapter by sharing my personal experience with the Holy Spirit. In 1983 I accepted Jesus as my Lord and personal Savior and was baptized in water shortly thereafter. I started attending church services each Sabbath (Saturday), and eagerly began learning about Jehovah. I was very excited about my new life and consumed the word of God voraciously. I was not baptized with the Holy Spirit as yet, but truly desired to be. I just wanted to desperately know the reality of Jehovah and not just believe it. I prayed fervently to be close to God and to have God close to me. Jesus became my world and my only focus.

I learned how to fast (denying yourself food and water for a specific period as a sacrifice to Jehovah), and fasted at least one day per week. I committed myself to reading the complete Bible from the book of Genesis to the book of Revelation and successfully did so in about a year and a half, and most importantly I started praying for the baptism with the Holy Spirit. Approximately two years after being baptized with water, as I knelt in prayer, I suddenly felt something enter my body from my legs. It started very slowly and moved up my legs, then my thighs, my torso and eventually my entire body. It was a very powerful presence and it took control of my entire being. I knew it was the Holy Spirit and suddenly, though I had already expressed my regret at having lived a sinful life before being saved and being baptized, a great feeling of sorrow for my past sins suddenly overwhelmed me and I began to weep. I wept uncontrollably for quite a long time at every memory of my past sins and could not be comforted. My tears, however, were not just for my sins but they were also tears of joy that I had been forgiven for all my offences.

My life from that point was never the same. I started experiencing a greater level of intimacy with Jehovah and started to deeply fall in love with Him. I kept on fasting and praying regularly and would not miss a single church service. Even when there would be no service at the church I requested and received permission so I could go into the sanctuary and pray.

I still was not baptized with the Holy Spirit, I knew this, but my first experience of knowing Jehovah is real and not just believing it enriched my spiritual and natural life tremendously. It was just a few weeks after this initial experience that the Holy Spirit came upon me and I was baptized with the Spirit of God. The power of God descended upon me on a Sabbath afternoon as my then pastor prayed for me to receive the baptism with the Holy Spirit just as we have seen in the previous texts from the book of Acts. The Holy Spirit took control of my entire body and I started speaking in an unknown tongue. I was inundated with the power of Jehovah and began experiencing a love that words cannot describe. My life has never been the same.

A few weeks after this experience, a friend of mine informed me that his mother had suffered a terrible stroke. She had been hospitalized and had been subsequently released from the hospital and sent home as there was nothing the doctors could do for her. She was completely paralyzed and could not speak. When I visited my friend's home (I visited with other members of the church), I saw how truly ill she was. She was only able to move her head. Her body was completely paralyzed.

I prayed for her believing that she would walk again and in my new found zeal informed the other brethren of the church that the Holy Spirit said that she would indeed walk that night. Sadly, of those that were with me that night, almost no one believed she would be healed. After praying for several hours nothing had changed. Most people left after a while but I remained. I was determined to see this woman out of her bed and walking before I would go home. I knew I had the power of the Holy Spirit in me and was determined to prove that Jehovah still did miracles.

A few more hours passed and by this time almost everyone had left and gone home as it was quite late at night. Suddenly the Holy Spirit came upon me and I began speaking in an unknown tongue. The Holy Spirit took control of my body, led me over to the paralyzed woman and I began lifting her by the hand while still speaking in an unknown tongue. Miraculously her body acquired strength, her paralyzed arms and legs began moving and I lifted her from her bed and she stood up on her feet. She was terrified and thought she would fall. I assured her she would not and asked her to walk after me as I led her by the hand like an adult leading a child. In just a few minutes she realized that she was not going to fall and started walking after me. Before I left that night, she was walking on her own without assistance throughout her house.

My friend later informed me that she was walking to and from the hospital that very week unassisted and refusing to take a cab. It was the first miracle I had witnessed and the first miracle Jehovah did through the Holy Spirit in me. I have witnessed many more miracles

since then; the miraculous healing of brain tumors, the restoring
of sight to failing eyes, the immediate removal of growths from the
bodies of patients, and the complete healing of cancers.

My greatest satisfaction with the miracles that Jehovah did
through me by the power of the Holy Spirit was when He granted
me the privilege of praying for my sick father. My father was an
unbeliever and one that held organized religion in disdain. He was
not pleased with me, to say the least, when I accepted Jesus and got
saved. He had become very ill and was hospitalized and in great pain. I
informed the pastor of my then church of his illness and a group was
organized to visit him in the hospital and pray for him. He allowed
us to pray for him and I assured him that God would heal him.

The following day I visited again and saw my dad in even more
pain. I was very disappointed as I thought surely he was going to
experience Jehovah's healing. His pain was unbearable and he told me
that I should never take anyone from my church to pray for him ever
again. I spoke to my dad softly and placed my hands on him and told
him I would pray for him and never again take any group to pray for
him. I prayed for my father and went home. I visited the following
day and as I entered the hospital room I saw my father sitting up
in bed and smiling. He pointed at me and said with delight, *"There
is something in you boy... there is something in you!"* He then explained
that after I prayed and left he suddenly fell into a deep sleep and
after awakening he said he had no pain. He was discharged from the
hospital the following afternoon as they found nothing wrong with
him. This was a miracle from the Holy Spirit.

The baptism with the Holy Spirit took my personal relationship
with Jesus to greater heights and to a depth of intimacy that I could
not have otherwise experienced.

7

Death, Burial, Resurrection, & The Coming Judgment

If sin and death did not exist, Jesus would not exist. Jesus is the manifested human form of Jehovah, who came to be because of the sins of humanity. Sin brought death into the world and as a result Jesus came to the earth to die as the spotless lamb of Jehovah, so that death can be defeated. Death was not a part of Jehovah's original plan for mankind. It is true to say that Jehovah did not create death, just as it is true to say that Jehovah did not create sin. Sin came through disobedience to Jehovah, and as a result of sin, death came into existence. It can be successfully reasoned that humans created death, a creation that came into being through mankind's experimenting with sin. Death is the Frankenstein that was created by Adam and Eve when they chose experimenting over obedience. Sadly their experiment did not go as planned and the monster called death has ravaged the human species since then.

There are two kinds of death. There is spiritual death and there is also natural death. Most of us are familiar with the latter and are fearful of the latter. Very few of us are aware of the former or even understand what it is. In this chapter we'll look at both natural and spiritual death in great detail. We'll also take a look at the antidote to both natural and spiritual death, the resurrection of all the dead, and finally we'll look at the coming judgment of all humankind, those that are alive and those that will be resurrected from the dead.

To understand natural death we'll go back to the beginning, that is, creation and the story of the fore parents of all mankind, Adam and his wife Eve. Adam and Eve were the first humans created by Jehovah. Even though our school systems now teach our children that we are all descended from Apes and that we evolved into humans over billions of years, the simple truth is that Jehovah created two humans named Adam and Eve. Adam and Eve were created to live forever in a world of splendor and beauty that was without sin. They were to have fellowship with Jehovah and they would have no material needs at all that were not met. Jehovah gave them authority over the earth and all the species of animals that exist on it and their home was a paradise called the Garden of Eden. Life was to be perfect. There was no pain, no sickness, no disease, no sorrow, and no death. They would live in an earthly paradise and they would live forever.

What more could they ask for?! They had been given all things; all things except one. There was a tree placed in the Garden of Eden, a tree called the *"tree of the knowledge of good and evil,"* and Jehovah instructed them to eat from all the trees in the Garden of Eden except this one. While this sounds fairly straight forward, there was another player present in the Garden of Eden that would make this a daunting task for the progenitors of the human family. This other character was Satan the devil, also known as the Serpent. Satan convinced the woman Eve that Jehovah was "holding out" on them. He convinced Eve that Jehovah was trying to deny them knowledge they had a right to and that Jehovah did not want them to fulfill their true potential in being exactly like Him.

Eve was sold! Her lust to have power was kindled and her desire to be a goddess was born. She was unconcerned with the fact that Jehovah had created her and that all she had was owed to Him. She was not thankful that He kept her fed, protected, innocent, and sheltered. Oh no! Jehovah was being unfair to her and her husband! He was keeping them from being gods.

Eve's desire to be like God led her to disobey God and her disobedience introduced sin and death to the world. The human body, which had been pure and perfect, now became sinful and vulnerable to sickness and disease. This body would no longer remain youthful forever, it would now grow old, weak, and feeble, and eventually it would die. This is called natural death; the death of the physical human body because of sin.

The human body could no longer live forever because sin brought with it many things that were by nature contrary to the personality and character of Jehovah. After all, it was still Jehovah's creation and despite the introduction of sin into the world, Jehovah was still Lord of the universe. The introduction of sin into the equation called life was an act of rebellion against Jehovah, orchestrated by Satan who used the vulnerable human female as a pawn in his rebellion against the Creator. If sinful mankind was allowed to live forever in their state of sin, then the rebellion against Jehovah would last for all eternity. To prevent this eternal rebellion, sin carried the consequence of death. Death would limit the time each individual would spend alive upon the earth.

As we've already seen in earlier chapters, the human being is not only a body, but a composite of a body and a human spirit. Both body and spirit results in what is called a soul. Thus the Holy Scriptures describe the living person as a living soul. The physical death of the human body does not result in the death of the human spirit; it results in a separation of the spirit from the body. The human spirit is the true person and the body is nothing more than the home of the spirit. Without the spirit, the body is dead, but the spirit continues to live even without the body. We've already seen this from the Holy Scriptures in earlier chapters of this book.

Natural death results in the destruction of the physical body. It is buried in the earth, it decays and is consumed by worms as it becomes a natural part of the earth once more. This is not true for the human spirit as it is not destroyed but goes to Jehovah to be judged. The human spirit is the true individual who is as conscious and as aware of being alive without a body as when he or she was alive within a body. Physical death does not result in a cessation of awareness and consciousness of the individual; it only results in a cessation of the functions of the physical body and an exiting of the physical realm for the individual.

Contrary to what the scientific community would have the world believe, we are not just created of matter and cease to exist after physical death. I often make the comparison between a human and a car to highlight the ridiculousness of stating humans are just physical matter. A car that has been left for many years unattended and uncared for and open to the elements will rust and eventually cease to function. That car however, can be brought back to function simply by replacing rusted parts and repairing the body of the car. It is done all the time and for collectors of vintage automobiles, it can be quite a profitable endeavor.

The same is not true for the human being. Human beings cannot be brought back to life to function regardless of what science does. Let's again take a look at our car. It may need to have the engine completely taken out and replaced after having "died" for many years. While this "dead" motor vehicle was languishing in someone's garage or probably in an open field with an unusable engine, the body of the car was rusting and the vehicle was falling apart. A collector of vintage automobiles may discover it and he or she will begin the process of restoring it and "bringing it back to life." This can be done no matter how long ago this vehicle was "dead."

A human being, however, if dead for even ten minutes cannot be brought back to life by humans. Even if hooked up to all the machinery of modern medicine, the individual cannot be brought back to life as the car was. If the individual died from a heart attack, once dead, a replacement heart (heart transplant) cannot restore life. Likewise if the individual died from lung cancer, once dead, a lung transplant will do no good. If humans were just matter, just as the car was restored after being "dead" for many years, surely life could be restored after death by making the necessary repairs. This is not the case, however, as the human being is not just made of physical matter but is a composite of physical matter and spirit. Once the human spirit and the human body have been separated through death, it is only Jehovah's power that can rejoin them to bring back life to the body.

While physical death results in the destruction of the physical body, spiritual death cannot be described as the destruction of the spirit of the individual. The Holy Scriptures informs us that physical death brings spiritual judgment and the consequences of this judgment have to be borne by the individual in either of two places, heaven or hell. Heaven and hell are literal places, not concepts created by the various religions of the world. The Holy Scriptures are very clear on this. The Holy Scriptures also make clear that there is a natural physical world, the world we see and experience around us, and then there is a spiritual realm, a world that exists around us but we cannot see it while living in our physical bodies.

Just as we cannot see spirits, we cannot see the spiritual world around us. Hell and heaven are literal places in the spiritual world. In fact they are the only two places that exist in the spiritual world. There is no third place called Purgatory. Purgatory is a fabrication and a falsehood and has not been mentioned in the Holy Scriptures even once. Spiritual death occurs to the individual who has lived a life without accepting Jesus as their personal Savior, has died in their sins, and has been sentenced to an eternal existence in hell.

It must be carefully noted that they do not cease to exist in hell but that they continue to exist there for eternity. Jesus describes hell as a place of fire and torment where maggots or worms do not die and the fire there never goes out. He also describes it as a place of thick darkness where there is great weeping and gnashing of teeth.

The Holy Scriptures further informs us that hell was prepared as a place of punishment for the devil, Satan and his angels and not for human beings. Human beings who live a sinful life without ever repenting of their sins and without accepting Jesus as their Lord and

Savior will spend an eternity there literally. This punishment is what is known as spiritual death.

Spiritual death is the eternal separation of the human spirit from Jehovah for all eternity in the literal place of torment called hell. It is described as death because it is forever and there is no hope or reprieve from this punishment and no hope of being reunited with Jehovah. For those who die in their sins, unsaved and without Jesus, they immediately enter this place of torment and will never be allowed out. To many this may sound like a tale of horror that has been dreamed up by organized religion to scare the unbelieving into being a part of a religious body or group. This is not the case. Individuals who live in fear of death and are not saved are not being irrational. They are not suffering from an irrational phobia that can be addressed and cured by some psychologist or psychotherapist. They are in fact justified in being fearful. Individuals that are living without Jesus as their Savior should in fact be afraid to die. They should be *VERY* afraid.

The death of the sinful, unsaved person is the beginning of horrors that cannot be described. Several years ago I met a woman in Pennsylvania who described to me her experience of witnessing the death of her aunt as she sat by her death bed. Her aunt was not saved, had not accepted Jesus as her personal Savior, and was not converted. She described to me the terrifying story of her aunt's ordeal as she passed from this natural world into a spiritual hell. She told me that while dying, her aunt started urgently requesting that they pull her up on the bed as she was slipping into the fire. She was screaming and asking her family members if they could not see the fire. She was pulled up on the bed until there was just no further place to pull her up. The woman told me that her aunt died screaming and with terror etched on her face. Her last words were about the fire she was slipping into.

This event so traumatized this woman that she said it opened her eyes to the reality of hell and she then gave her life to Jesus and was a born again Christian at the time of our meeting.

There are many who will dismiss this story and will attribute the fire this woman was seeing to hallucinations. There are also those who will try to explain it away with scientific or psychological concepts of what happens to the brain while a person is dying and will declare such occurrences as normal to the process of death. This however is not true. Science cannot explain what science has no way of proving. Science has no authority in matters that relate to the spirit as science is empirical, that is, science can only authoritatively address what it can prove through observation or experimentation.

The scientific community's view on what occurs at death can best be described as guess work as they cannot die themselves and return to explain what occurs at death, and this would be the only valid experiment that would lend authority and credibility to their views. Jesus, on the other hand, has great authority on the subject of life and death, and heaven and hell. You see, Jesus actually died and came back! Since Jesus actually died and was resurrected He is in a position to speak to us credibly about death.

Since He created heaven and also hell, He is in a position to tell us about hell and why it was created. No member of the scientific community has these credentials. No one should be consoled by the scientific community's view that the individual ceases to exist at death as Jesus contradicts this and He is the only authority on the subject.

Conscious awareness exists beyond death and the spiritual person is still alive after the physical body has died.

There is another interesting story of a sickly asthmatic woman that attended the church I was baptized in. I was not very close to her but my wife knew her very well and was in fact very close to her and her daughter. The story of her final days was related to my wife by her daughter who witnessed her death as she sat by her bedside. This sweet old lady was always in and out of hospitals because of her asthma, so no one was alarmed when she was admitted to the hospital after suffering another asthma attack. She was expected to be out again in just a few days.

Her daughter visited her in the hospital, expecting that she would be discharged from the hospital very soon. She said her mom was visibly well at the time of the visit and was sitting up in her hospital bed. As she conversed with her mother, the young woman informed her that the doctors would be sending her home very soon, to which her mother responded that she would not be going back home. Puzzled by her mother's response, she asked her mother what exactly she meant. Her mom responded with a question, *"Can't you see them? Can't you see the angels coming for me?"* The daughter responded, *"No mom, I can't see them."* Her mom then began singing Gospel songs, told her daughter goodbye, closed her eyes, and fell asleep singing. She died right before her eyes, knowing she was being taken to heaven.

This old, asthmatic woman had been a born again Christian for many years and at the point of her death, when the spirit begins separating from the body, she could see heaven, her spiritual destination and place of her eternal reward.

There are millions of people dying each day. Many are born again Christians who are saved and many millions more are not. There are many horror stories that can be told about people dying without Jesus and there are also many beautiful stories of people dying knowing that they will be with Jesus in heaven. What is common to both the believer in Jesus and the unbeliever is that in both cases the body dies. After the death of the body, however, all similarities end. Hell greets the unsaved with eternal death and heaven greets the saved with eternal life.

For the unsaved who have not accepted Jesus as Lord and Savior and are still skeptical about what happens after death, I recommend the watching of the VHS tape or DVD of *"To Hell and Back"* by Dr. Maurice Rawlings. It documents the accounts of several people who suffered what is known as clinical death, which is death before rigor mortis sets in, and were resuscitated. Their stories of seeing hell and all its torments is enough to convince the most skeptical.

The Holy Scriptures speak of the resurrection from the dead. In fact it speaks of two separate resurrections from the dead. It also tells of a final judgment that shall occur at the end of this current world. The world will not continue on as a drunken sailor being tossed about by the violent and evil actions of humans. Sorrow, suffering, disease, and death will not always reign supreme in the earth. The world as we know it will soon come to its end.

The Holy Scriptures foretells of the triumphant return of Jesus to the earth, not as a lamb to be slaughtered, but as the judge of the earth. Jesus will return to the earth and will impose order upon the earth through His divine rule from the New Jerusalem. He will rule the earth in peace for one thousand years. During His reign, Satan will be bound, and all nations and peoples will acknowledge His kingship and will worship Him as King of Kings and Lord of Lords. There will be no option besides worshipping Jesus. This is recorded in the book of Romans, *"…As I live, saith the Lord, every knee shall bow to me, and every tongue shall confess to God" (KJV, Romans 14:11)*

At the time of Jesus' return to the earth, the believers that are still alive will be taken up from the earth to meet Him in the sky and the saints that are dead will be resurrected from the dead to meet Him also. This future event is recorded in the New Testament book of I Thessalonians, *"Our Lord Jesus told us that when he comes, we won't go up to meet him ahead of his followers who have already died. With a loud command and with the shout of the chief angel and a blast of God's trumpet, the Lord will return from heaven. Then those who had faith in Christ before they died will be raised to life. Next, all of us who are still alive will be taken up into the clouds together with them to meet the Lord in the sky. From that time on we will all be with the Lord forever."(CEV, 1 Thessalonians 4:15-17)*

During this time of Jesus' earthly reign, the saints of Jehovah that were dead, that is, those that had accepted Jesus as Savior and were saved at the time of their death, shall be resurrected to life to rule with Him for the thousand years of His reign. They will be resurrected with new spiritual bodies that cannot die that are just like Jesus' body. The saints that were alive will also receive new spiritual bodies.

People that are alive and unsaved will be ruled over by the saints in the kingdom of Jesus for the thousand year period and Satan will be bound for the thousand year period. This is described in the Holy Scriptures as the first resurrection and is outlined in the book of Revelation:

"I saw an angel come down from heaven, carrying the key to the deep pit and a big chain. He chained the dragon for a thousand years. It is that old snake, who is also known as the devil and Satan. Then the angel threw the dragon into the pit. He locked and sealed it, so that a thousand years would go by before the dragon could fool the nations again. But after that, it would have to be set free for a little while. I saw thrones, and sitting on those thrones were the ones who had been given the right to judge. I also saw the souls of the people who had their heads cut off because they had told about Jesus and preached God's message. They were the same ones who had not worshiped the beast or the idol, and they had refused to let its mark be put on their hands or foreheads. They will come to life and rule with Christ for a thousand years. These people are the first to be raised to life, and they are especially blessed and holy. The second death has no power over them. They will be priests for God and Christ and will rule with them for a thousand years. No other dead people were raised to life until a thousand years later."(CEV, Revelation 20:1-5)

The first resurrection will be the resurrection of the saints, that is, those that are saved. The unsaved will not be resurrected at this time but will be resurrected after the one thousand years reign of Jesus upon the earth. After this one thousand year reign, the unsaved will be resurrected to face their final judgment before the judgment seat of Jesus. All the unsaved that were being tormented in hell since the time they died will be brought back to life and given a spiritual body of death. They will then receive formal judgment by Jesus for all the things they did during their lifetime and their fate will be sealed to spend eternity in a lake of fire with the devil and all his demonic followers.

This is known in the Holy Scriptures as the second death and is recorded in the following verses of the book of Revelation, *"And I saw a great white seat, and him who was seated on it, before whose face the earth and the heaven went in flight; and there was no place for them. And I saw the dead, great and small, taking their places before the high seat; and the books were open, and another book was open, which is the book of life; and the dead were judged by the things which were in the books, even by their works. And the sea gave up the dead which were in it; and death and Hell gave up the dead which were in them; and they were judged every man by his works. And death and Hell were put into the sea of fire. This is the second death, even the sea of fire. And if anyone's name was not in the book of life, he went down into the sea of fire."(BBE, Revelation 20.11-15)*

The second resurrection and the final judgment will bring an end to this world of sin forever. The unsaved along with Satan and his demonic spirits will spend an eternity in the sea of fire. Hell will no longer exist as a place the unsaved dead go to as there will be no more unsaved people. All the people will be the people of Jehovah. Sin will finally cease to exist; there will be no more death, no more violence, no more hate, no more hunger, no more disease, and no more suffering upon the earth. The earth will be made new and Jesus will have complete dominion over the earth and the universe. There will be no more separate nations as the earth will exist finally as one nation under Jehovah.

For those of us who have accepted Jesus as Lord and Savior and are living in His righteousness, the news of the second coming of Jesus and the final judgment sends waves of delightful thoughts through our minds and spirits. To those that are unsaved this news is not greeted with the same level of enthusiasm. The good news, however, is that everyone can be saved. Jesus died so that salvation is available to everyone as a free gift. Death and the prospect of hell do not have to reign over humanity. The terror and dread that accompanies the thought of dying and spending an eternity in hell does not have to be. Jesus offers us a way out, a way out that has been purchased by His own blood. I lived for many years with the fear and dread of dying and going to hell, but accepting Jesus and being born again liberated me from this dread. Being certain that your eternity is one of peace, joy, and happiness will deliver everyone from the fear and dread of death and hell.

If the Holy Spirit is speaking to your heart to be saved as you read these words, simply stop and ask Jesus to forgive you of your sins, ask Him to come into your heart, and ask Him to be your Lord and Savior. He will come into your heart and He will lead you to salvation and liberation from fear and the tyranny of death. Seek to be baptized and give up your life of sin and you will be converted. Keep the commandments of Jehovah and worship and love Him with all your heart. This will guarantee you a place in the first resurrection, a place in heaven, and a place in the Kingdom of Jehovah when the earth is made new and the devil is no more.

8

The Catholic Religion

In this chapter we'll take a look at Christianity and the Catholic religion. This is important as to truly define Christianity and the path to salvation through Jesus Christ, we must also identify religions that closely resemble Christianity but which, by the definition of Christianity outlined in earlier chapters, are not. To remind ourselves of that definition, we stated earlier that the Christian religion is based on the teachings of Jesus the Christ, the son of the living God, Jehovah, as outlined in the Holy Bible. The Holy Bible includes both the Old and New Testaments and no other book. Based on this definition we are therefore authorized to state that Catholicism is not Christianity and has never been. It is in fact a different religion created in Rome under the auspices of the Roman Emperor Constantine and perpetrated throughout the world as Christianity. Roman Catholicism needs to be closely looked at so that those seeking salvation through Jesus will not be misguided into embracing this religion while believing that they are embracing Christianity when in fact they are not. It is important to state very clearly that Catholicism and Christianity are two distinct and separate religions. This is true from the perspective of the Holy Scriptures.

Even though Catholicism has paraded under the banner of Christianity and for many centuries has called itself *"the Church,"* it is not the religion created by Jesus Christ and the Apostles of Jesus. One of the inevitable consequences of discovering truth is that falsehoods are always identified in the process. This is why truth must be clearly defined and the source of truth clearly identified. It has been made clear from the first chapter of this book that the source of truth and the only reference that is used for truth for the Christian religion and this book is the Holy Bible. No other source or reference is considered truth as far as the salvation of humanity is concerned.

Jesus is the only way to salvation and the Holy Bible is the only source for His words and those of Jehovah that can lead to everlasting life. It is within this context that we'll look at the Catholic religion and it is from this perspective that we'll identify the great differences between Catholicism and Christianity. We'll look at the founding of Catholicism vis-à-vis the founding of Christianity and we'll also look at some fundamental differences in doctrines between the two. The Papacy will be looked at along with the various titles of the Pope and several Catholic religious practices and rituals will be examined.

To understand the Catholic religion, we'll need to educate ourselves briefly with Roman history and with an Emperor referred to by historians as Constantine the Great. Constantine is credited with making the Christian religion a legal religion throughout the then Roman Empire. Although he was not actually the first Roman Emperor to grant legal status to the Christian religion, he is credited with the same because he not only granted legal recognition to it but actually promoted and favored Christianity as the religion of the Empire.

Born Gaius Flavius Valerius Aurelius Constantinus, it is said that he credited the Christian God with his military victory at the battle of the Milvian Bridge on October 28, 312, over a much stronger opponent. This victory made him sole ruler of the Roman Empire. Tradition has it, that as he marched into battle, he had a vision of a cross appearing before the sun along with two Greek letters, chi (X) and rho (P), the first two letters of the Greek word that means Christ. He also saw the inscription in Greek, "Εν τούτω Νίκα", En Touto Nika, meaning "with this win," which is translated into Latin to read "In hoc signo vinces," meaning "in this sign thou shalt conquer."

Constantine went on to unify the Roman Empire under his sole political leadership and also went on to unify the citizens of Rome under one religion, *his* newly minted version of Christianity. It is important to point out that he more or less created his own version of the Christian religion, which became known as Roman Catholicism, as he authorized that the first day of the week, Sunday was to be observed as the Christian Sabbath, instead of the seventh day weekly Sabbath outlined in the Holy Scriptures and observed by Christians at the time.

He convened and presided over several *"Christian"* councils including the First Council of Nicaea, which was called to discuss the nature of Jesus relative to Jehovah. Constantine was anti-Semitic (this is believed to be one of the reasons he rejected the Sabbath as he wanted nothing in common with Jews) and during his reign passed several laws against Jews. He used derogatory language in describing Jews and laid the foundation for centuries of hostilities and persecutions against Jews by the Roman Catholic Church. Theodoret, a Christian bishop and author who lived between the years 393 - 457 records in his Ecclesiastical History I.9, the Epistle Emperor Constantine addressed to those bishops who were not present at the First Council of Nicaea, regarding the dates of Easter and that of the Passover:

*"It was, in the first place, declared improper to follow the custom of the Jews in the celebration of this holy festival, because, their hands having been stained with crime, the minds of **these wretched men** are necessarily blinded.... Let us, then, have nothing in common with the **Jews, who are our adversaries**. ... avoiding all contact with that evil way. ... who, after having compassed the death of the Lord, **being out of their minds, are guided not by sound reason, but by an unrestrained passion,** wherever their **innate madness** carries them. ... **a people so utterly depraved**. ... Therefore, this irregularity must be corrected, in order that we may **no more have any thing in common with those parricides and the murderers of our Lord**. ... **no single point in common with the perjury of the Jews**."*

Eleven years prior to his death he had his eldest son executed upon a rumor that his son was having an affair with his second wife and a few months later had his wife executed when he found out she was the source of the original rumor.

He held the title Pontifex Maximus, the same title the Pope holds today and which means Supreme Pontiff. He was most assuredly the first Pope of the new religion he had created although the Roman Catholic Church denies this and has falsely declared that the Apostle Peter was the first Pope. The Pontifex Maximus was the high priest of the Ancient Roman *College of Pontiffs* and was the most important position in ancient Roman Pagan religion. The Apostle Peter was never a pagan and never a part of the College of Pontiffs.

Peter was a Jew who was called by Jesus and became a Christian and leader of the Christian church in Jerusalem. The *Collegium Pontificum* or College of Pontiffs was an ancient Roman religious body whose job it was to keep the pagan gods of the Empire happy and it was composed of the highest-ranking priests of the Roman pagan state religion. At the head of this body was the *Pontifex Maximus* or Supreme Pontiff also known today as the Pope.

Constantine was not baptized or converted and was reportedly still a sun worshipper until the day of his death. He was purportedly baptized, that is, water was poured upon his head, while lying upon his death bed and it is reported that he referred to himself as the thirteenth Apostle. Constantine died in the year 337. Thus Constantine's reign as Emperor of the Roman Empire gave birth to what is now known as the Roman Catholic religion, a religion created through the merging of ancient Roman pagan religions and practices with a perverted version of Christianity that forbade the observing of the seventh day or weekly Sabbath in favor of Sunday, a day dedicated to the sun god.

Constantine can be appropriately credited with the founding of this religion, Catholicism, which was founded approximately four centuries *after* Christianity was established by the Apostles of Jesus. The Apostle Peter most assuredly was not its founder and neither was he its first Pope.

Christianity has never had a Pope and the only Holy Father known to the Christian religion is Jehovah. There has never been a College of Pontiffs in the Christian church and the title Pontifex Maximus is unknown to the Christian church. These are all pagan titles and positions which have been borrowed from ancient Roman pagan religions that have been merged with the Catholic religion created by Constantine the Great.

The birth of the Roman Catholic religion holds great religious, prophetic, and historical significance. First we see the Roman political system hijacking the Christian religion, forbidding the seventh day weekly Sabbath as they wanted nothing to do with the Jews, and then placing a political figure, the Roman Emperor, at its head. We then see the merging of ancient pagan religions with this new found Catholic religion, and we also see the emergence of anti-Semitism among its leaders. The most significant development, however, was the political backing and investment of resources that was received by this new religion from the Roman political machinery. This unprecedented political and economic backing for a state religion resulted in the creation of a rival religion to Christianity that unlike the true Christian church, which had been persecuted for centuries, it now received the favor, resources, and blessings of the Roman Empire. The new religion was labeled Christianity and called *the Church*, even though it was not, in an effort to deceive and confuse those seeking the true way of salvation. In short order the Catholic religion grew into one of the world's most powerful political and quasi spiritual organizations and in time eclipsed the power of the Roman Empire itself, becoming the most powerful force to contend with on the face of the earth. The Pope, the head of this organization, then became the most powerful man on the earth and the Papacy became the most powerful office that could be occupied.

Popes assumed many titles to reflect the growing importance of the Papacy and also made many claims such as that of infallibility. Among the many titles assumed were *Bishop of Rome* and *Vicar of Jesus Christ, Vicar of Peter, His Holiness the Pope, The Holy Father, Successor of St. Peter, Prince of the Apostles, Pontifex Maximus* (High Priest), *Supreme*

Pontiff Of The Universal Church, and *Servant Of The Servants Of God*. The word *"Vicar"* is derived from the Latin word *"Vicarius"* which means *"agent for someone superior or to act in the person of."* Thus the title *"Vicar of Jesus Christ"* means the Pope is acting in the person of Jesus and the title *"Vicar of Peter"* means the Pope is acting in the person of the Apostle Peter.

These titles reflected the belief in the Catholic religion that the Papacy was bestowed with divine authority over all matters on earth and in heaven. This belief led to various outrageous claims by the Papacy which placed the Popes above being mere human beings. Here are just some of the claims made by the Papacy regarding the authority of Popes:

1. *"The Pope is of so great dignity and so exalted that **he is not mere man, but as it were God**, and the vicar of God."*

2. *"The Pope is crowned with a triple crown, **as king of heaven and of earth and of the lower regions.**"*

3. *"The Pope is as it were **God on earth**, Sole sovereign of all the faithful of Christ, **chief king of kings**, having a plentitude of unbroken power, entrusted by the omnipotent God to govern the earthly and heavenly kingdoms."*

4. *"The Pope is of so **great authority and power, that he is able to modify, declare, or interpret even divine laws.**"*

There is also the claim of Papal infallibility and the issuing of statements by the Pope *"ex-cathedra,"* which literally means *"from the chair,"* and refers to *"divine"* teaching on morals and doctrine issued by the Pope that are deemed equivalent to any teaching or doctrine found in the Holy Scriptures.

The following are a few examples of such "ex-cathedra" statements or teachings that are considered to be as infallible as the Holy Scriptures:

1. *"There is but one universal Church of the faithful, outside of which no one at all can be saved"* (*Pope Innocent III, Fourth Lateran Council, 1215.*)

2. *"We declare, say, define, and pronounce that it is absolutely necessary for the salvation of every human creature to be subject to the Roman Pontiff"* (*Pope Boniface VIII, the Bull Unam Sanctam, 1302.*)

3. *"[The Holy Roman Church] firmly believes, professes and teaches that none of those who are not within the Catholic Church, not only Pagans, but Jews, heretics and schismatics, can ever be partakers of eternal life, but are to go into the eternal fire 'prepared for the devil, and his angels..."* (*Mansi, Concilia, xxxi, 1739.*) (*Pope Eugene IV, The Bull Cantate Domino, 1441*).

It is clear to anyone who has ever read the Holy Scriptures that these *"infallible"* statements are purely falsehoods and that the Catholic Church does not have any authority in determining who will be saved and who will spend an eternity in the fires of hell. It is also a falsehood that *"every human creature"* needs to be subject to the Roman Pontiff in order to receive salvation. Salvation is a free gift given by Jehovah through His son Jesus Christ and has nothing at all to do with the Papacy. Jesus is the only authority on salvation and it is to Jesus that we all must submit ourselves. It is also evident from these claims and ex-cathedra *"infallible"* statements that the Papacy and Catholicism fall outside the realm of the Christianity outlined in the Holy Scriptures as no such authority has been vested upon any mere mortal.

The Pope is just another sinful human being just as all other human beings are. In fact it is necessary to point out that Popes need to be saved themselves as they are not in compliance with the Holy Scriptures. While they claim authority over heaven, Earth, and the Underworld as represented by the Triple Crown, the history of the Papacy is a sordid tale of licentiousness, murders, anti-Semitism, torture, rape, and mass killings. This is not surprising, however, as the religion was not founded on the teachings of Jesus and the Apostles or on the doctrines contained in the Holy Scriptures. Catholicism was instead given birth to by the cruelest of Empires that have ever existed, the Roman Empire, and was nurtured by pagan Roman doctrine from its state religions. From its inception, the Christian doctrines found in the Holy Scriptures were never seriously regarded and its priests and bishops, beginning with Constantine, saw no need to adhere to the Gospel of Jesus.

Unlike the Roman Catholic religion, Christianity was founded by Jesus Christ and spread by the preaching of His twelve Jewish Apostles. It never had a College of Pontiffs, a Supreme Pontiff or Pope, and was never anti-Semitic. The Apostles never claimed infallibility and as seen before, the Apostle Paul painfully outlined in the book of Romans, his struggle with his flesh. There were no divine claims of authority over heaven, Earth, and the Underworld by any of the followers of Jesus, and they heaped no great titles upon themselves, such as *"Vicar of God"* or *"Vicar of Christ."* There was no anti-Semitism in the churches as all the early Christian churches were Jewish and the Gospel of Jesus had to be preached to the Jews first. It was only through the call of the Apostle Paul and his commission to take the Gospel to the Gentiles that the Gospel was finally preached en masse unto the Gentile peoples.

Christianity is a pro-Jewish religion as outlined in the New Testament book of Romans and is built on the foundation of the Jewish people. Both Old and New Testament books of the Bible are written by Jewish Prophets, Priests, Kings, Judges, and Apostles. The Bible is in fact a Jewish book. Jesus was Jewish as were all the Apostles that preached the Gospel.

All the earlier churches were established by Jews and converted Gentiles were even described as spiritual Jews. The Apostle Paul in writing about those who are truly Jewish describes the converted Gentile in this manner, *"The true Jew is not one who is only so publicly, and circumcision is not that which may be seen in the flesh: But he is a Jew who is a secret one, whose circumcision is of the heart, in the spirit and not in the letter; whose praise is not from men, but from God."(BBE, Romans 2:28-29)*

Here the Apostle describes Gentile believers as being spiritual Jews who are not circumcised in the flesh but in the heart. Christianity has never been an anti-Semitic religion and was never established upon an anti-Semitic foundation. It could not be as its founder and source is Jewish.

There are many notable differences in doctrine between what the Holy Scriptures teach and what the Catholic religion practices and advocates. The following four Catholic practices and doctrines are considered worthy of mention:

1. The Worship of the Virgin Mary

2. Offering prayers to "Saints"

3. Bowing before idols and images in prayer

4. The use of the Rosary

The worship and the offering of prayers to the Virgin Mary are not sanctioned in the Holy Scriptures and are in fact condemned in the Holy Scriptures. There is no record in the Holy Scriptures of anyone acknowledging Mary for more than what she was; she was just a woman chosen by Jehovah to give birth to His son Jesus. She has nothing divine about her, has no special powers, was not selected to do or be anything special in the newly established church, and was not worshipped by any of the Apostles of Jesus. Jesus left the Apostles no special instructions regarding her and her role in the church and it is clear from the Holy Scriptures that she was treated as just another member of the church led by the Apostle Peter.

The practice of offering prayers to Mary is idolatrous and came about as a result of the continued worship of the goddess Ishtar, mentioned in previous chapters of this book. Ishtar, also known as the Queen of heaven, was an ancient pagan deity that has been worshipped by many ancient pagan civilizations including pagan Rome. To continue her worship under the Catholic religion, she was dubbed the Virgin Mary to facilitate her continued worship under the new Catholic religion.

It is noteworthy that the Virgin Mary is still called the Queen of heaven in Catholic prayers, just as Ishtar is known. The Holy Scriptures inform us that Jesus is the only way to Jehovah and without Him no man or woman can be saved. We are admonished in the scriptures that we should pray to Jehovah in the name of His son Jesus. There is no mention of Mary. Despite this, the Catholic religion has dubbed her *"The Mother of God," "The Blessed Virgin Mary,"* and the *"Queen of Heaven."* Prayers are offered to her and millions of people around the world bow down before statues and images of her.

Jesus has clearly stated that He and He alone is the way to Jehovah. Praying to Mary, besides being an absolute waste of time, is an offence to Jehovah. Here again is what Jesus said, *'"I am the way, the truth, and the life!"... "Without me, no one can go to the Father..."'* (CEV, John 14:6) and again He states in the book of John, *"And whatsoever ye shall ask in my name, that will I do, that the Father may be glorified in the Son."* (KJV, John 14:13)

It is made clear by Jesus that **ALL** prayer must be done in His name. There is no mention of Mary! Jesus also stated in the book of Matthew that Jehovah is the **ONLY** person to be worshipped, *"...it is written, Thou shalt worship the Lord thy God, and him only shalt thou serve."*(KJV, Matthew 4:10)

We are permitted to worship Jesus only because Jesus is the manifested physical presence of Jehovah as we have already seen. Jesus and Jehovah are one and the same. To worship Mary is the same as making her another god and Mary was just an ordinary woman who was selected for an extraordinary task by Jehovah. She received salvation through the same process that we all have to go through to receive salvation. She was baptized, born again, and converted. She was a part of the church founded by the Apostles and was saved through the grace offered her by the Almighty God. She should not be worshipped, bowed down to, or prayed to. She is not a goddess and truly is in no position to assist anyone on earth seeking salvation. The following prayer is often repeated by practicing Catholics:

Hail Mary, full of grace.

Our Lord is with thee.

Blessed art thou among women,

and blessed is the fruit of thy womb, Jesus.

Holy Mary, Mother of God,

pray for us sinners,

now and at the hour of our death.

Amen.

It is called the Hail Mary prayer and is repeated over and over by Catholics. It is my duty as a born again believer to inform all Roman Catholics and anyone who has repeated this prayer that Mary is in no position to pray for anyone's sins and cannot help anyone at the time of death. No one should invest their faith in such a prayer as it is absolute folly to seek the help of Mary and not that of Jesus. Mary cannot assist anyone, cannot hear anyone's prayer, and cannot intervene at the hour of death to offer salvation to anyone. Jesus is the only source of help, of life, and of salvation.

Another practice that often occurs during the saying of prayers to Mary is the bowing down of the Catholic believer to a statue, an image, or some makeshift alter dedicated to Mary. This brings us to the other Catholic doctrine of bowing down to images and idols. The bowing down to idols and images is a pagan practice that is strictly forbidden by Jehovah in the Ten Commandments and throughout the Holy Scriptures. The commandment forbidding the bowing down to idols is recorded in the book of Exodus and is the second of the Ten Commandments, *"Do not make idols that look like anything in the sky or on earth or in the ocean under the earth. Don't bow down and worship idols." (CEV, Exodus 20:4-5)*

Bowing down to images of Mary or images of anyone or anything during prayer and worship is a violation of this commandment and is idolatry. Idolatry is a grievous sin before Jehovah and is vehemently condemned throughout both the Old and New Testament books of the Bible. Statues of Jesus, the Apostle Peter, the Apostle Paul, and the Virgin Mary often adorn Catholic churches and many people are seen bowing before these statues in prayer and in worship. This is a non-Christian idolatrous practice that predates Christianity. This practice, however, was very common in pagan Rome and was incorporated into the Catholic religion at the creation of the religion by Constantine.   The Holy Scriptures warns us to stay away from idols. This is recorded in the New Testament book of I John, *"Children, you must stay away from idols"* (CEV, 1 John 5:21) and also the book of 2 Corinthians, *"Do idols belong in the temple of God? We are the temple of the living God, as God himself says, "I will live with these people and walk among them. I will be their God, and they will be my people." The Lord also says, "Leave them and stay away! Don't touch anything that isn't clean. Then I will welcome you."* (CEV, 2 Corinthians 6:16-17)

Statues have no place in a Christian church and the practice is not supported by the Holy Scriptures. Praying before a statue constitutes an act of idolatry, it is also a violation of the commandment of Jehovah, and offers no benefit to the believer as statues cannot hear or respond to prayers.

Just as statues cannot hear or respond to our prayers, the same is true for those that are dead and are declared saints. The practice of praying to saints is not supported by the Holy Scriptures. The Catholic religion has a process for making dead men and women into saints. The problem with this practice, however, begins with the process. The Holy Scriptures inform us that all born again and converted Christians are the saints of Jehovah and there is no authority given to an earthly institution to make anyone a saint.

The word *"saint"* and *"saints"* occurs many times throughout the scriptures and is often used in reference to those believers that are alive upon the earth. King David of Israel wrote in the book of the Psalms that the saints should sing unto the Lord, *"Sing unto the LORD, O ye saints of his, and give thanks at the remembrance of his holiness." (KJV, Psalms 30:4)*, he also advises that the saints should love the Lord as it is Jehovah who preserves and rewards them, *"O love the LORD, all ye his saints: for the LORD preserveth the faithful, and plentifully rewardeth the proud doer." (KJV, Psalms 31:23)*

It is clear from these scriptures that saints are believers in Jehovah who follow Him in obedience and do not have to be dead to be saints. The Apostle Paul also makes numerous references to the saints in his many writings to the early church. He addresses the born again believers as the saints of Jehovah. In the following verse taken from the book of Romans, the Apostle states that he is on his way to Jerusalem to minister to the saints, *"But now I go unto Jerusalem to minister unto the saints." (KJV, Romans 15:25)* The saints he refers to here are the believers that are in Jerusalem. The notion that saints are dead men and women that are in heaven and have somehow qualified for *"sainthood"* through miraculous deeds after death is a falsehood. All true believers in Jehovah and His son Jesus, who are converted and are in obedience to His commandments, are saints. The Catholic institution cannot make anyone, dead or alive, a saint.

A saint does not become one after death as all born again believers that are genuinely converted and are living in the righteousness of Jehovah are His saints. There is no process that needs to be recognized and followed for a believer to become a saint except that which is already outlined in the Holy Scriptures. Dead saints are not to be worshipped or prayed to. This is a pagan form of worship and violates the commandments of Jehovah.

No one should pray to the Apostle Peter, the Apostle Paul, the Virgin Mary, any of the dead Popes, or any other Catholic saint. This is a foolish practice for the following reasons:

1. The dead person being prayed to cannot see or hear the prayers being offered and cannot answer them.

2. As seen before in earlier chapters, the spirit of the dead person is immediately judged by Jehovah and is either in the place of torment called hell or with Jesus in the place called Paradise in heaven. No one except Jesus and Jehovah knows exactly where the spirit of the person is and even though we would all hope our loved ones are all in heaven, this is just not the case.

3. Praying to the dead constitutes worship and is an offence to Jehovah.

Jesus informs us that many people who expect to be in the kingdom of God will not be as they were not obedient to the commandments of Jehovah. Jesus states this very clearly in the book of Matthew and informs us that obedience to the commandments of Jehovah is the criteria for entering, *"Not everyone who calls me their Lord will get into the kingdom of heaven. Only the ones who obey my Father in heaven will get in. On the day of judgment many will call me their Lord. They will say, "We preached in your name, and in your name we forced out demons and worked many miracles." But I will tell them, "I will have nothing to do with you! Get out of my sight, you evil people!" Anyone who hears and obeys these teachings of mine is like a wise person who built a house on solid rock." (CEV, Matthew 7:21-24)*

It is clearly not enough to be sincere and religious to enter the kingdom of God and it is also clear that no religious organization can authorize anyone's entry into heaven. As seen from the verses quoted, many preachers, and workers of miracles will not be allowed entry. Jesus will reject them as unrighteous and evil and they will spend an eternity in the fires of hell as seen before. It is important to point out at this juncture that the praises of men, their awards, and their accolades do not constitute the righteousness of Jehovah and cannot influence His decision to allow anyone into His kingdom or into Paradise.

The Catholic religious organization may elevate dead men and women, sing their praises, document their many acts of goodwill, and declare them saints that are in heaven, however, they have no way of knowing where they are. If they were not born again believers who lived according to the commandments of Jehovah as outlined by the Holy Scriptures they are not in heaven and no one can place them there. Since it is true that we cannot tell where the spirits of the dead are, how can we pray to those spirits? The person being prayed to may just be in hell crying out for the mercies of God that are no more accessible. Given this reality, isn't it utterly foolish to pray to *"saints?"* The saint that is being prayed to may just be a sinner that is being tormented in a hell that is all too real.

We'll now look at the rosary and why it should not be utilized as a means of communicating with Jehovah in prayer. It must be first stated that the rosary extends the idolatrous practice of worshipping the Virgin Mary, a practice we've already looked at and have seen from the Holy Scriptures that it is in violation of the commandments of Jehovah.

The rosary is described as a devotion in honor of the Virgin Mary. There are a set number of specific prayers the believer has to say over and over at a set number of times. There is also what is called *"Mysteries"* to be meditated upon and at the end of the rosary there is a prayer to the Virgin Mary. The order of praying by the rosary is outlined below:

1. Make the Sign of the Cross and say the *"Apostles' Creed."*

2. Say the *"Our Father"*

3. Say three *"Hail Marys"*

4. Say the *"Glory be to the Father"*

5. Announce the *First Mystery;* then say the *"Our Father"*

6. Say ten *"Hail Marys"* while meditating on the Mystery

7. Say the *"Glory be to the Father"*

8. Announce the Second *Mystery* and Say the *"Our Father"*

9. Repeat ten *"Hail Marys"* and say the *"Glory be to the Father"*

10. Continue with *Third, Fourth and Fifth Mysteries*

The following prayer to Mary is said after the rosary is complete:

"HAIL, HOLY QUEEN, Mother of Mercy, our life, our sweetness and our hope! To thee do we cry, poor banished children of Eve; to thee do we send up our sighs, mourning and weeping in this valley of tears. Turn then, most gracious advocate, thine eyes of mercy toward us, and after this our exile, show unto us the blessed fruit of thy womb, Jesus. O clement, O loving, O sweet Virgin Mary!"

Also below is the text of what is called the Apostles' Creed:

The Apostles' Creed

"I believe in God, the Father Almighty, Creator of heaven and earth; and in Jesus Christ, His only Son, our Lord; Who was conceived by the Holy Spirit, born of the Virgin Mary, suffered under Pontius Pilate, was crucified, died, and was buried. He descended into hell; the third day He arose again from the dead. He ascended into heaven, and sits at the right hand of God, the Father Almighty; from thence He shall come to judge the living and the dead. I believe in the Holy Spirit, the Holy Catholic Church, the communion of Saints, the forgiveness of sins, the resurrection of the body and life everlasting. Amen."

As seen from the rosary outline, there are a number of repetitions of "Hail Marys" and the "Our Father" along with meditation on various "Mysteries." The prayer at the end of all the repetition and meditation is an appeal to Mary, who is addressed as "Holy Queen" and "Mother of Mercy," and instead of crying to Jesus, the prayer cries out to Mary for mercy! The sad truth is that so many millions of people around the world are engaged each day in the repeating of these meaningless prayers and are calling out to Mary for mercy and salvation. Mary can neither hear these prayers nor is she in a position to respond to them.

Jesus also cautioned us not to use repetition in our prayers and describes these repetitions as vain, "But *when ye pray, use not vain repetitions, as the heathen do: for they think that they shall be heard for their much speaking." (KJV, Matthew 6:7)*

It was the practice of the heathen nations to repeat prayers over and over again in the belief that by repeating the prayers they will be heard by their gods. Christians are asked to have a conversation with Jehovah as children approaching a loving father. We make our requests known to Him in prayer, offer our praises to Him in prayer, and develop a genuine, intimate relationship with Him based on conversation. Walking around with rosary beads and vainly repeating *"Hail Marys," "Our Father,"* various *"Mysteries,"* and *"Glory be to the Father"* will not build a relationship with Jehovah. The rosary honors Mary, is worship to Mary, and is a pagan, heathenish practice that Jesus voices disapproval of.

Conclusion

The writing of this book has been a labor of love; love for my family, my friends, and love for lost humanity. Jesus demonstrated His love for mankind by dying on a cross so that our sins would be forgiven and that we could inherit eternal life through believing in Him. I attempt to demonstrate my love through the writing of this book, and in telling all who read it about Jesus' sacrifice for them. It is my hope that many who will read this book, which contains not only my personal experiences but also information about salvation from the Holy Bible, will yield their hearts unto Jesus our Savior and be saved.

The current state of the world is frightening. There are wars everywhere, famines stalk entire continents, and there is great hopelessness, great fear, widespread religious deception, and the absence of trust in societies across the globe. Selfishness and cruelty seem to be at an all time high with rape, kidnappings, physical, mental, and verbal abuse being dished out to children all around the world. The evening news on television is enough to send one into depression and despair. Marriages are failing at record rates and homosexuality has suddenly exploded onto the stage of our everyday existence with every other person "coming out."

Children have also grown cruel and loveless as they reflect the world that they live in. School shootings have become common; children are killing their own parents, killing their neighborhood playmates, and scheming to commit even more heinous crimes against society. The world seems to have gone mad with over indulgence in all the vices. Safety seems a thing of the past as we are forced to imprison ourselves in our homes with electronic security systems and more and more households are acquiring personal hand guns in an effort to bring some sense of safety to the home. The response to all these concerns from the world's governments is often corruption and incompetence.

There is also a great spiritual void, an emptiness that is being experienced by so many who have long realized that material possessions and physical pleasures offer no satisfaction to their inner most longing; the longing for peace, hope, and the assurance that life is not just an empty wasteland of carnal pleasures, vice, and violence. This book is a response to those who say to themselves, *"There must be more to life than this."* There is indeed more...a lot more. Jesus died to introduce humanity to true life and to true spiritual personal satisfaction. He states the reason for His death, burial, and resurrection clearly throughout the Holy Scriptures and made clear to all humanity that He died not for His sins, but for ours.

Jesus, the sinless lamb of Jehovah became sin for humanity so that we could escape the penalty of sin and enter into eternal life.

In the book of John 10:10, Jesus says, *"I came so that everyone would have life, and have it in its fullest."(CEV)* Jesus came to demonstrate to us the reason we were created and why we are here upon the earth. He also came to deliver us from the fear of eternal death in a literal place called hell, and He came to give us hope and peace that we cannot find outside of Him. No one has to live in fear and hopelessness and no one has to dread the thought of dying and being uncertain about what occurs after death. This book outlines what Jesus taught concerning living as God designed life to be. It also opens our eyes to the hope that lies beyond the grave and it tells how to walk in the righteousness of Jehovah that will ensure we are all saved.

Jesus tells us that the truth would liberate us from all the traps the enemy Satan has designed for us. He states, *"You will know the truth, and the truth will set you free." (CEV, John 8:32)* Only truth can liberate us in mind and spirit, and only truth can guarantee us peace and security. You have been presented with the truth of the Holy Scriptures, and it is my hope that the truth of Jesus will be embraced to set you free.

We want to hear from you.
Let us know how this book has
impacted you. Please send your
comments about this book to us in
care of contact@beulahoutreach.org.
Thank you.

754752

Made in the USA